# About the Author

Mrs. Sandy Paul has 10 years of experience Java. Her has worked on large banking projects in tier-1 Software Companies in India, USA, UK, Australia and Switzerland.

Her hobbies include travelling to new tourist places, watching basketball, cricket and learning latest technological stuff.

## Preface

This book is for those who want to learn the basic concepts in JAVA. I have covered all the important concepts in Java as mentioned below.

1. Java Introduction
2. Java Language specification
3. Basic of Java
4. Data Types ans Variables
5. Important packages and Classes
6. Modifiers in Java
7. Conditional statements in Java
8. Loops in Java
9. OOPS concepts
10. Characers
11. Boxing and Unboxing In Java
12. Number conversion and casting
13. Arrays
14. Command line arguments
15. variable Number of arguments
16. Exception Handling
17. String Handling
18. Mathematical Operations
19. Date and Time
20. Regular Expressions
21. Input output programming
22. Nested Classes
23. Collection

# Table of Contents

# 1. Java Introduction

## 1.1 Background

Java is a widely used programming language in the world. Syntax of Java matches with that of C++.

Java is one of the most popular languages in the world. Billions of computers, mobile phones and other electronic devices use Java.

## 1.2 Striking features of Java

1. Object oriented
2. Automatic memory management using garbage collection
3. Supports multi-threading
4. Platform independent
5. All Java programs are executed in JVM (Java Virtual Machine)
6. Developed by James Gosling @ Sun Micro system (Now Oracle) in 1995

## 1.3 Installation and Environment Set up

You can check if the Java is installed or not in your system using below command in windows.

***>java –version*** in command prompt.

```
C:\Users\sagar>java -version
java version "1.6.0"
Java(TM) SE Runtime Environment (build 1.6.0-b105)
Java HotSpot(TM) Client VM (build 1.6.0-b105, mixed mode, sharing)
```

Figure 1 - Java Command

If you get the output as shown in figure, that means you have already java installed in your system. But if you get error saying Java is not recognized as internal or external command, Then you will have to install jdk in your system.

To install jdk you can visit below url
http://www.oracle.com/technetwork/java/javase/downloads

After you install Java, again try to run above command. This time you will see the correct output.

After you download eclipse in zip format, you will have to unzip it. Folder structure of the eclipse after unzipping is shown in previuos figure.

To launch eclipse, you will have double click on the eclipse.exe file.

To execute Java programs, you need JRE – Java Run time Environment. But to write and compile java source code, you will need JDK – Java development kit. When you install JDK, JRE is automatically installed.

## 1.4 How to set up Java in Windows

1. Download the JDK from Oracle download page. Depending on your system, you will download 32 bit or 64 bit exe file.

2. Once the exe file is downloaded, just double click on that file and follow on-screen instructions to install JDK.
3. Then You will have to configure some important Java environment variables as mentioned below.

Configuring the Java Environment Variables – There are several Java Environment variables that you must configure as mentioned below. Just open Environment variables window and add these variables.

1. JAVA_HOME : C:\Program Files\Java\jdk1.7.0_79
2. JDK_HOME : %JAVA_HOME%
3. JRE_HOME : %JAVA_HOME%\jre
4. CLASSPATH : .;%JAVA_HOME%\lib;%JAVA_HOME%\jre\lib You can also give the path of other directories where java class files exists.
5. PATH : Just append %JAVA_HOME%\bin to the value of PATH Variable. Be careful. DO NOT overwrite this variable's value. Otherwise your system might not work properly.

Below images will guide you through Java Environment Variables configuration process in Windows.

## Step 1 – Open Advanced System Settings from Control Panel

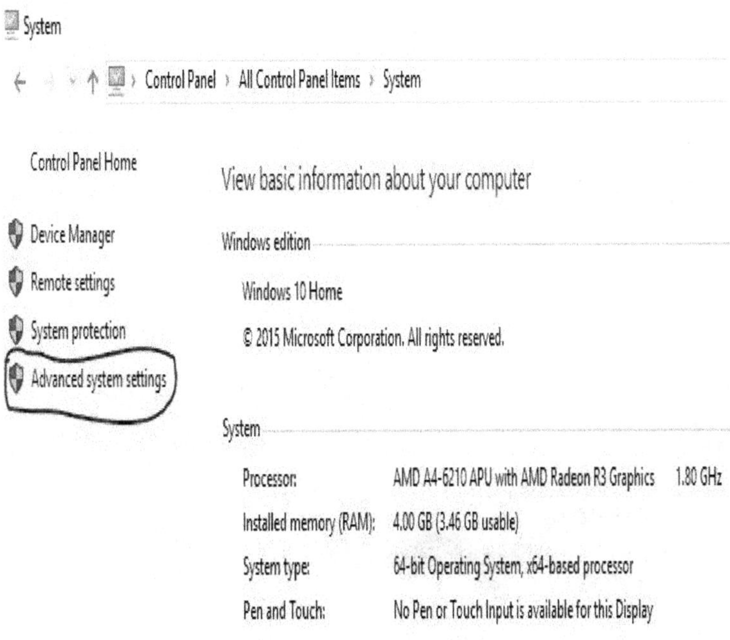

Step 2 – Click on Environment Variables Button

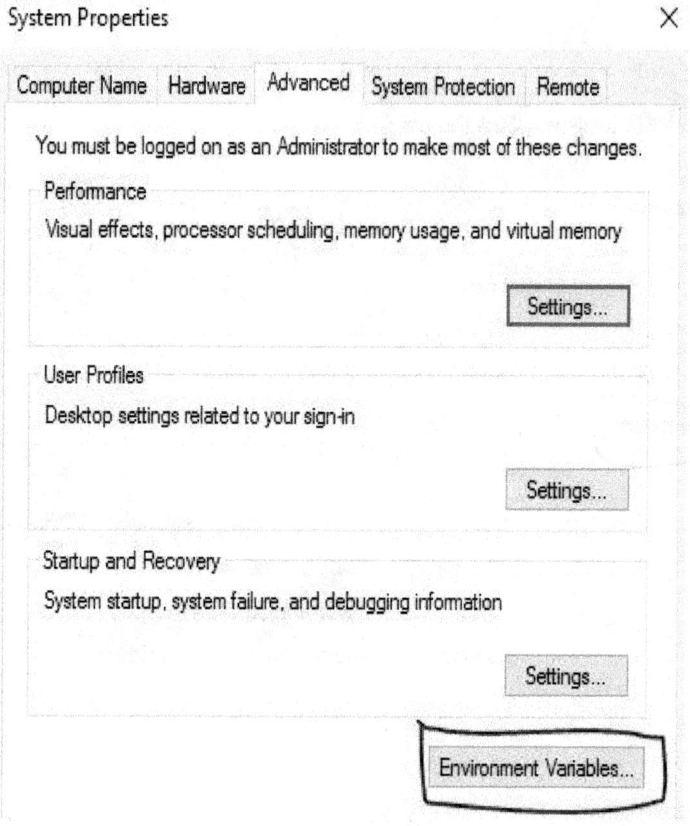

Step 3 – Add Java Environment Variables as shown in below image.

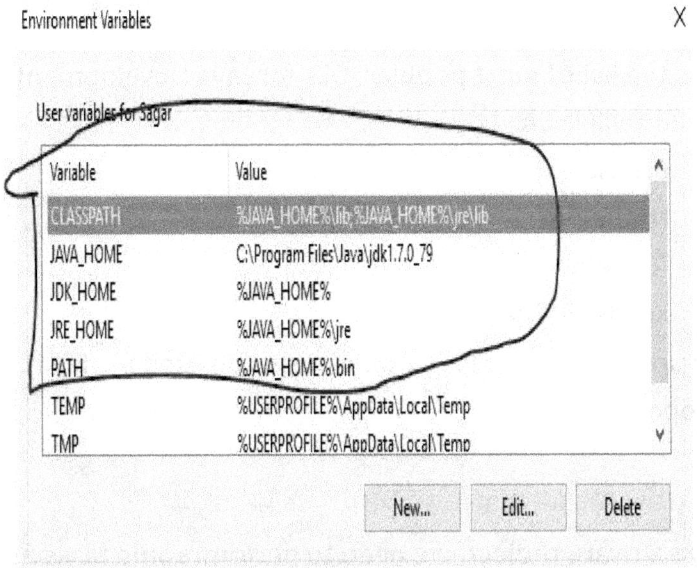

## 1.5 IDE for JAVA development

To develop Java applications, you will need IDE – Integrated Development Environment.

Here is the list of most popular IDEs for Java Development.

1. Intellij IDEA
2. Eclipse
3. NetBeans
4. JDeveloper
5. Xcode on Mac OSX

There are some other IDEs that can also be used for Java development.

## 1.6 Build management tools in Java

In any software project, we need to perform some tasks as mentioned below.

1. Cleaning the environment
2. Compiling the source code
3. Compiling the test code
4. Executing the tests on CI server
5. Packaging the application
6. Deploying the application on the server

Doing all these tasks manually is tedious process. So that's when build management tools come in to picture. All tasks mentioned above can be automated using build tool.

Popular build management tools in Java are mentioned below.

1. Make
2. Ant
3. Maven
4. Gradle

# 2. Java Language specification

In this post, you will learn all important aspects of Java.

## 2.1 Key features of Java

1. It's an object oriented language.
2. Everything is Class and Object in Java.
3. Class, Interface and Enum names should start with Upper Case letter.
4. Package names should be in lower case.
5. Method names should start with lower case letter and each subsequent word should start in Capital letter – for example setMarks()
6. All Java statements end with semi-colon (;).
7. Single line Comments can be marked using // . For multi-line comments you need to use /* ..................*/

## 2.2 Keywords in Java

Here is the list of Keywords in Java.

1. Data types – int, float, byte, char, double, boolean, long, short
2. Access Modifiers – public, private, protected
3. Object Oriented – class, Object, interface, enum, extends, implements, import, instanceof, new, native, package, super, this
4. Other modifiers – static, abstract, strictfp, synchronized, transient, volatile,const, final

5. Constructs – break, case, continue, default, do, else, if, for, goto, switch, while
6. Exception related – catch, finally, throw, throws, try
7. Others – void, false, null, true, false, assert, return

## 2.3 Operators in Java

Here is the list of Operators in Java.

1. Arithmetic operators +, -, /, *, %, ++, —
2. Logical Operators ||, &&, !
3. Relational Operators <. >, ==, <=, >=, !=
4. Bitwise Operators &, |, ^, ~, <<, >>
5. Assignment Operators =, +=, -=, *=, /=, %=, <<=, >>=, &=, |=, ^=
6. Conditional operator ?:

Operator precedence – When calculating the mathematical expressions, Java uses operator precedence rule to calculate the final value of the expression.

For example – * operator has high precedence over – operator.

x = 5-2*9

Result of above expression would be 13 and not 27. If you want to override this rule, you can use parenthesis ().

x = (5-2) * 9

Result of above expression would be 27 as everything inside parenthesis is evaluated first.

## 2.4 Identifiers in Java

Identifiers are nothing but the names given to variables, methods, classes, interfaces etc. Here are the rules to define the identifiers in Java.

1. It should start with letter, _ or $
2. It can not contain any other special character like +, &, / etc
3. It should not have spaces in it

# 3. Basics of Java

## 3.1 First Program in Java

Now let us start with the coding. In this section, we will write a simple Java program.

You can follow below steps.

- Open Eclipse and create new Java Project.
- Create a package and class.

Below images will give you the idea of how to create a project in Eclipse.

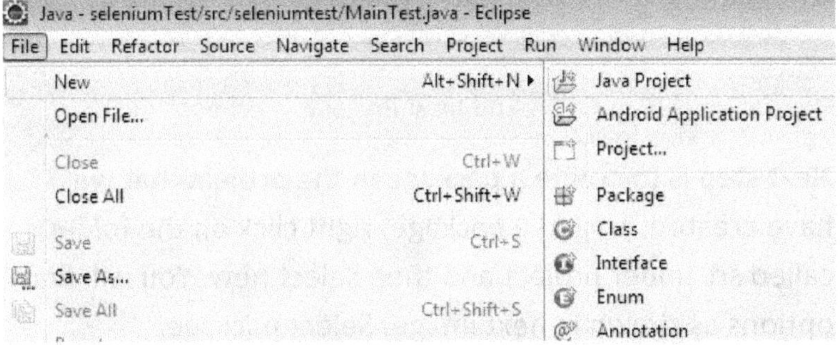


Figure 2 - Add New Java Project in Eclipse

In File menu, you have to click on new and then click on the Java Project. In new Java project window you will have to enter the name of the project and select the JRE.

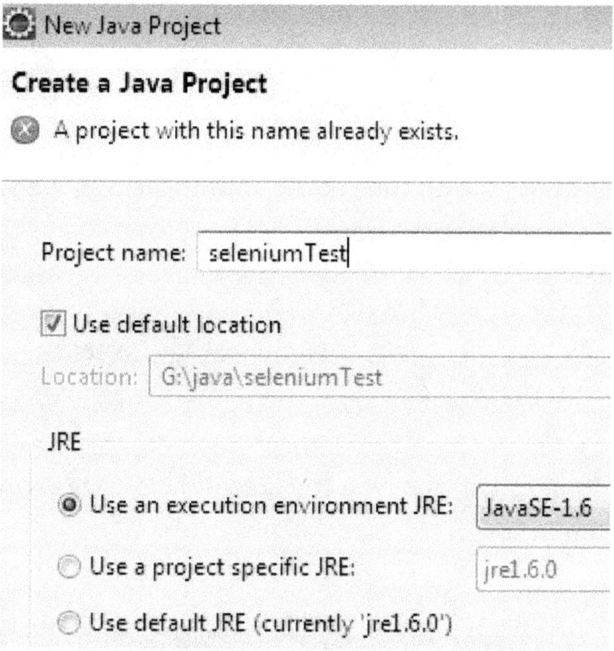

Figure 3 - Add new Project in Eclipse

Next step is to create a package in the project that we have created. To add a package, right click on the folder called src under project and then select new. You will find options as shown in next image. Select package.

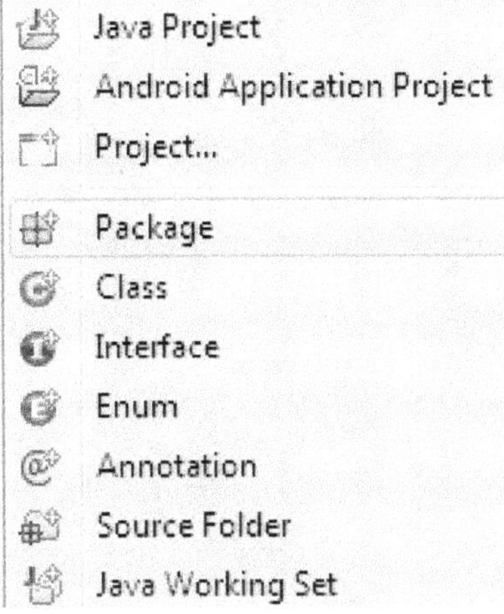


Figure 4 - Add new package

After you click on the package, you will see new package window. You will have to enter the name of package. As a convention, package names should be in small cap letters.

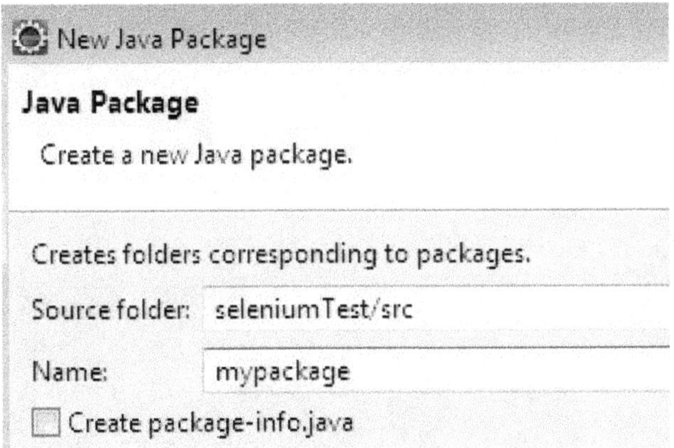


Figure 5 - Provide the name of package

Now you can add Java class, by right clicking on the package you have just added.

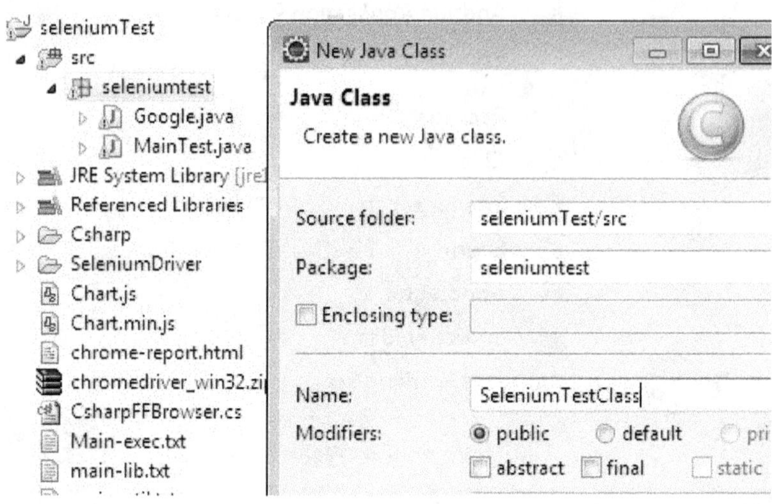


**Figure 6 - Add new Java Class**

In new Java class window, you will have to enter the name of class. As a convention, first letter of class name should be in upper case. When you click on finish, sample class code will be automatically created for you as shown in next image.

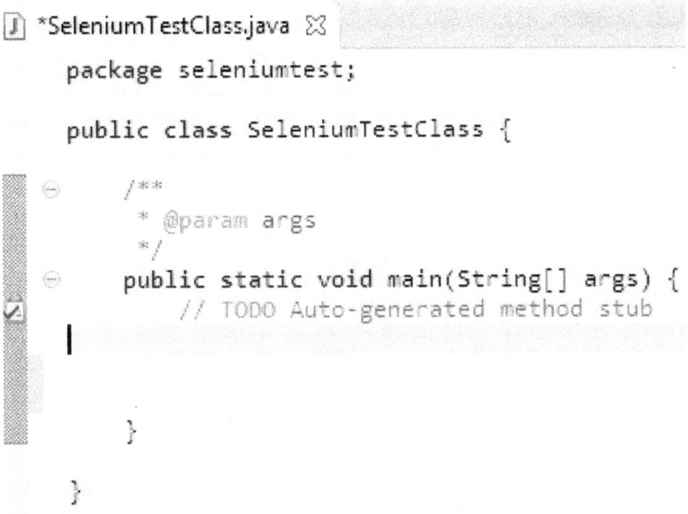

*SeleniumTestClass.java

```
package seleniumtest;

public class SeleniumTestClass {

    /**
     * @param args
     */
    public static void main(String[] args) {
        // TODO Auto-generated method stub


    }

}
```

Figure 7 - Sample Java Class Code

Now it is time to write some code in the main method and run the java program.

I have added just one line of code in the main method as shown in next figure.

System.*out*.println("First Java program in Eclipse");

Above line will print the string passed in as a parameter. To run the code, you will have to click on the run button (green ball button containing white arrow). To debug the code, you will have to click on the button looking like bug.

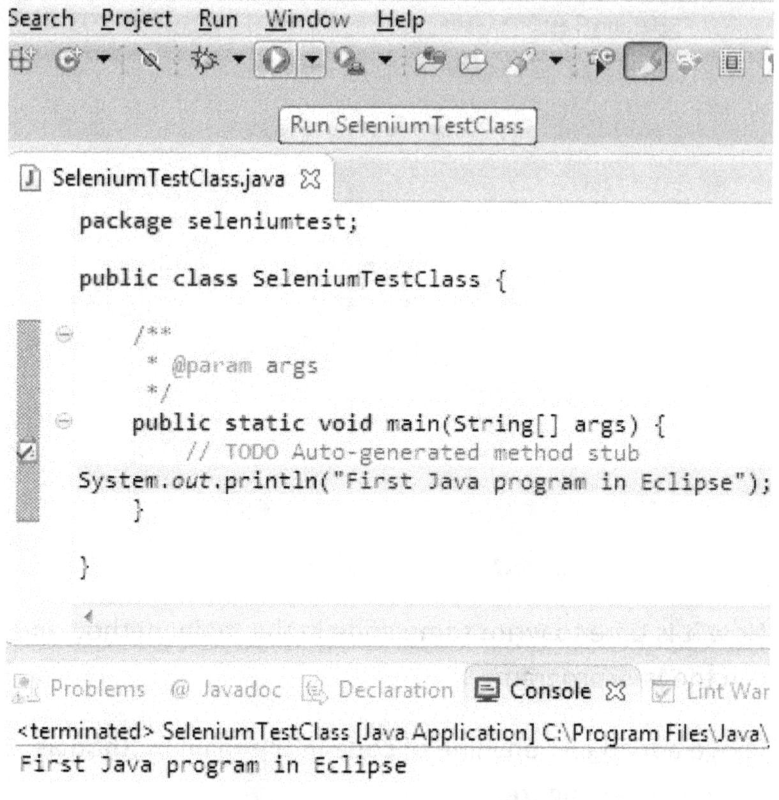


**Figure 8 - Running a Java Code**

After you run the program, you can see the ouput in the console window.

In this topic, we will learn below topics.

1. Writing first Java program
2. Compiling the program using IDE, javac
3. Executing the program using IDE, java
4. Debugging the program
5. Looking at output

Here is the simple Java class – Basic.Java

```
package simple;

/**
 * Created by Sagar on 16-04-2016.
 */
public class Basic
{
    public static void main(String [] args)
    {
        System.out.println("Hello
www.softpost.org");
    }

}
```

## 3.2 Compiling the Java class.

To compile the Java class file, you need to execute below command.

javac simple/Basic.java

Above command creates class file called Basic.class.

## 3.3 Running the Java class

To run the Basic.class file, you need to execute below command. Notice that you should be in the parent directory of simple (package directory) when running below command. Also note that how we access the class name. Since the class is in simple package, you need to access it using simple.Basic

Another important thing to note is that -cp switch. It tells JVM that classes can be found in current directory. If you do not pass correct class path, you will get error saying – could not find or load main class simple.Basic

```
java -cp . simple.Basic
```

**Here is the output of the code**

Hello www.softpost.org

## 3.4 Debugging the Java source code

Different IDEs provide different ways to debug the code using breakpoints. For example – Intellij IDEA allows us to add breakpoints, step into, step out of the break point.

# 4. Data Types and Variables

## 4.1 Data Types

There are 2 types of data types in Java.

1. Primitive
2. Reference (for example – string and objects of classes)

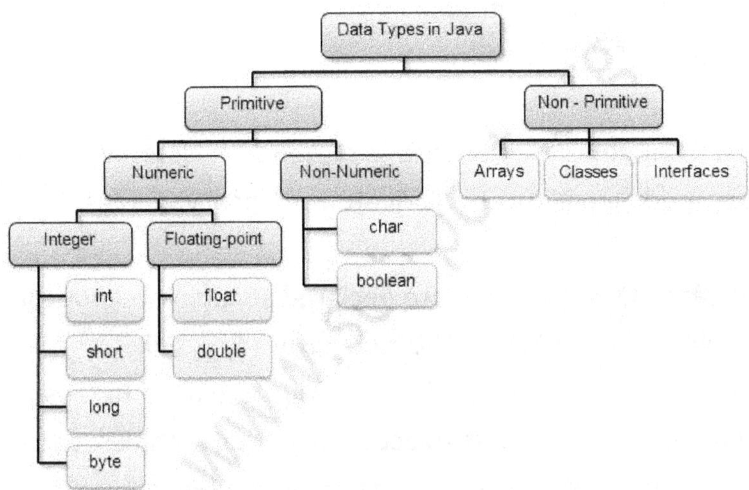


There are 8 primitive data types in Java.

Here is the list of primitive data types in Java.

1. boolean
2. short
3. int
4. float
5. double
6. long
7. char
8. byte

Remember that String is not a primitive data type. String is a class in Java and Strings are immutable meaning they can not be changed.

## 4.2 Variables

In Java, there are 3 types of variables.

1. Local
2. Instance Class variables
3. Static Class variables

Local variables are declared in methods of class. We can't use modifiers like public/private with local variables.

Instance Class variables are declared at class level outside of all methods of class. We can use modifiers like public/private with instance variables. We need to create the objects of the class to access instance variables. Each object gets it's own copy of instance variable in heap.

Static Class variables are declared at class level outside of all methods of class. We can use modifiers like public/private with instance variables. We can directly access static class variables using Class name. We do not need object of the class to access static variable. All objects share the same static variable.

# 5. Important packages and Classes

All classes in Java standard library are important but here is the list of frequently used packages and classes.

1. java.lang – This package is imported by default in all Java classes. It contains basic classes required to run a simplest program. Some of the most frequently used classes in this package are – String, Integer, Double etc
2. java.util – contains classes for Calendar, Date,Regular Expression related classes and various collections like List, Vector, Map, Dictionary, Set, Queue, Stack etc
3. java.io and java.nio – This package has got classes to interact with file system. java.io is used when dealing with stream oriented and blocking input output. While java.nio is used when dealing with buffer oriented and non blocking input output.
4. java.net – This package contains classes required to access resources over network and internet
5. java.awt and javax.swing – GUI applications
6. java.text – formatting of numbers and strings
7. java.applet – creating applets that run in browser

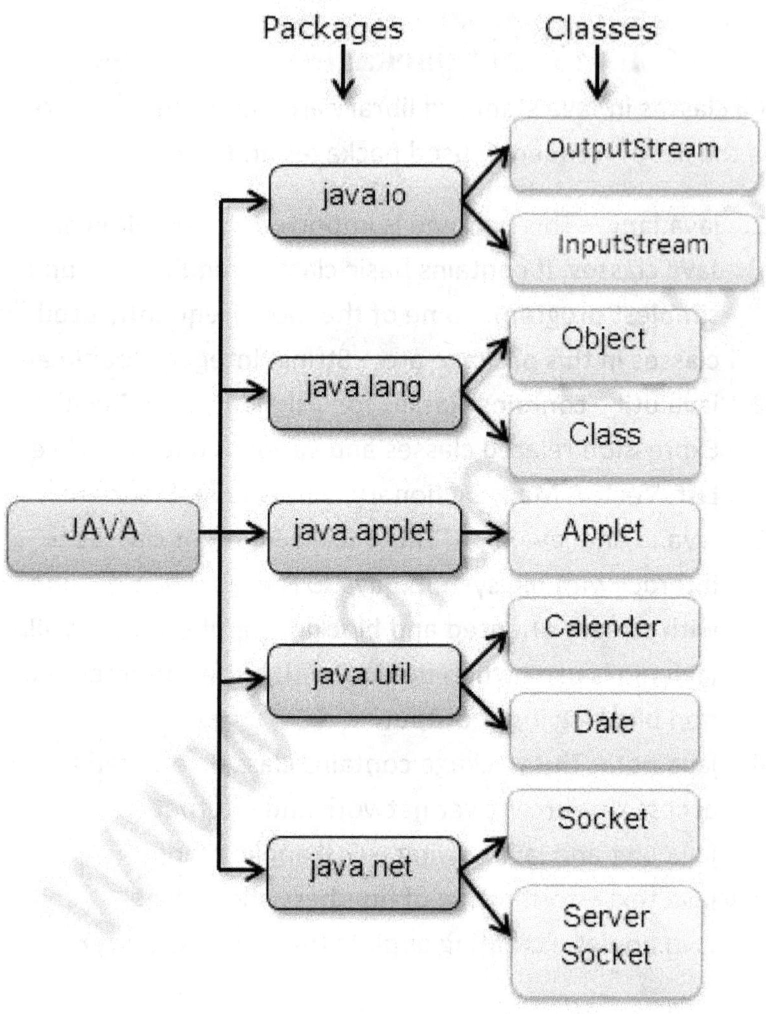
Packages
Classes
JAVA
java.io
java.lang
java.applet
java.util
java.net
OutputStream
InputStream
Object
Class
Applet
Calender
Date
Socket
Server Socket

# 6. Modifiers in Java

Modifiers are used to give special meaning to class, interface, fields or methods.

There are 2 types of modifiers in Java.

1. Access type of modifiers – used to specify the access level
2. Non-access type of modifiers – used for various purposes

## 6.1 Access Type modifiers

1. public – Public members can be accessed from outside of class.
2. default – This is the default access level. These members can be accessed from all classes within the same package.
3. protected – Protected members can be accessed from outside of class but the condition is that class from which you are accessing it should extend the main class.
4. private – Private members can not be accessed from outside of class. Only methods of class can access it from within the class.

Below example illustrates how access modifiers work. We have 2 classes. Account class is in package modifiers while SimpleTest class is in otherpackage.

```
package modifiers;
public class Account
{
    private double balance;
    protected String accountType;
    public String name;
    String address;
    public Account()
    {
        this.balance = 0;
        this.accountType = "Savings";
        this.name = "XXX";
        this.address = "Brisbane";
     }
    public void withDrawAmount(double amount)
   {
        this.balance = this.balance - amount;
    }
    public void depositAmount(double amount)
   {
        this.balance = this.balance + amount;
   }
    public double getBalance()
   {
        return balance;
   }
}



package otherpackage;
import modifiers.*;
public class SimpleTest
{
    public static void main(String args [])
   {
        //Account class is in modifiers package.
This class (SimpleTest) is in otherpackage.
        Account a = new Account();
        //accountType has a protected access -
compilation error
        //as we are accessing protected member from
different package
```

```
        //System.out.println("account type is -> " +
a.accountType);

        //Can not access the private member from
outside of class Account
        //balance has a protected access -
compilation error
        //System.out.println("account type is -> " +
a.balance);
        //We can access public members
        System.out.println("Name of the account is -
> " +  a.name);
        System.out.println("Balance of the account
is -> " +  a.getBalance());
        a.depositAmount(111);
        System.out.println("Balance of the account
after depositing 100 is -> " +  a.getBalance());
        a.withDrawAmount(11);
        System.out.println("Balance of the account
after withdrawing 11 is -> " +  a.getBalance());
        //We can not access address field of
modifiers.Account class from this package
        //System.out.println("address of the account
is -> " +  a.address);
    }
}
```

**Here is the output of above code.**

```
Name of the account is -> XXX
Balance of the account is -> 0.0
Balance of the account after depositing 100 is -> 111.0
Balance of the account after withdrawing 11 is -> 100.0
```

## 6.2 Non access Type modifiers

1. static – static members can be accessed using Class name. We do not need to create an object of the class to access static members.
2. final – final variables can be assigned value only once. final methods can not be over-ridden.
3. synchronized – Synchronized methods are used when we want thread safety.
4. transient – Transient variables are used when you do not want to store them in a file through serialization process. In short, they are temporary.
5. strictfp – we can mark class or method as strictfp to get the consistent results across different platforms in operations involving floating point arithmetic.

Below example explains how to use various non-access modifiers.

```
package modifiers;

/**
 * Created by ssalunke on 19/04/2016.
 */

public class NonAccessModifiers
{
    public static void main(String [] args)
    {
        //static, final, abstract, synchronized,
volatile, transient
        //We can access static method and variables
using class name
        //We do not need to create objects of
classes to access them
```

```
        A.printStatic();
        System.out.println("Value of size " +
A.size);
        A a1 = new A();
        //Below line will throw compilation error
saying
        //Can not assign a value to final variable
count
        //a1.count++;

        //Another thread will not be allowed to
invoke this method simultaneously
        a1.changeName("New Name");
    }
}

class A
{
    static int size =10;
    final int count = 1;
    String name;
    //Transient variables will not be saved during
serialization process
    transient int temp;
    //Variable d is volatile which means that d will
be read and written to main memory
    //and not from cpu cache
    volatile double d;
    public static void printStatic()
    {
        System.out.println("This is static method @
class level");

    }

    final void printFinal()
   {
        System.out.println("This is final method. Do
not try to override");
        //Below line will throw compilation error
saying
        //Can not assign a value to final variable
count
        //count++;
```

```
    }
    //This method is synchronized which means it is
thread safe
    synchronized public void  changeName(String
name)
{
        this.name = name;
    }
}

class B extends A
{
    //Below line will throw compilation error saying
    //Can not override printFinal as it is final
method
    //public void printFinal(){ }

}
```

**Here is the output of above code.**

```
This is static method @ class level
Value of size 10
```

# 7. Conditional statements in Java

There are 3 types of conditional statements in Java.

1. if.....else
2. Conditional operator ?:
3. switch

## 7.1 If...else

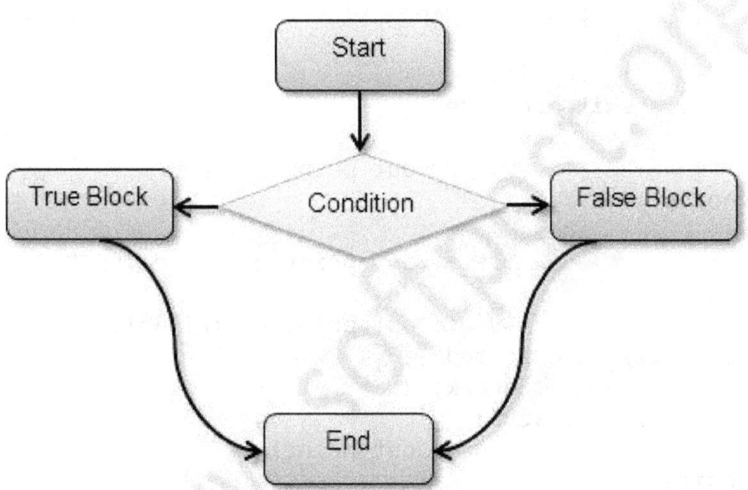


As show in above figure, if ...else construct is used to execute the sepecific block based on the outcome of the condition. If the condition is true, true block is executed. Otherwise false block is executed.

Below Java example illustrates how we can use conditional constructs in Java.

```
package conditional_statements;
/**
 * Created by Sagar on 16-04-2016.
 */
public class Conditionals {
    public static void main(String [] args){
        int a=13,b=11,c=2;
        if (a > b)
        {
           System.out.println("a is bigger than b");
        }
        else
        {
           System.out.println("a is less than b");
        }
        int choice=2;
        switch(choice){
            case 1:
                System.out.println("Choice is " +
choice);break;
            case 2:
                System.out.println("Choice is " +
choice);
                System.out.println("This block of
code will be executed");
                break;
            case 3:
                System.out.println("Choice is " +
choice);break;
            default:
                System.out.println("Choice is
default");

        }
    }
}
```

**Here is the output of above code.**

```
a is bigger than b
Choice is 2
This block of code will be executed
```

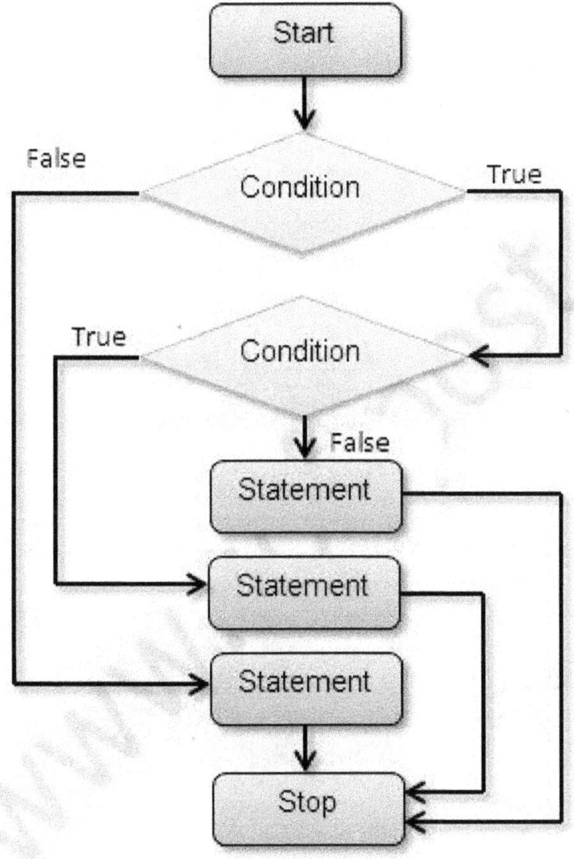

```
package Basicclass;
import java.io.*;
public class Basicjava
 {
	public static void main(String[] args)
	{
		int no;

		BufferedReader br=new
BufferedReader(new InputStreamReader(System.in));

		try
		{
		 System.out.println("Enter Number");
		no=Integer.parseInt(br.readLine());

		if(no%2==0)
		{

		  System.out.println("Number is Even");

		}
		else
		{
		   System.out.println("Number is Odd");
		}

		}
		catch(Exception e)
		{}
	}
}
```

## 7.2 Conditional Operator ?:

Below example illustrates use of conditional operator.

```
package conditional_statements;
/**
 * Created by Sagar on 19-04-2016.
 */
public class Condition
{
    public static void main(String args [])
    {
        int a = 10;
        //normal if condition
        boolean result ;
        if (a%2==0)
        {
            result = true;
        }
        else
        {
            result = false;
        }
        System.out.println("Result is -> " +
result);
        //based on outcome of condition, assignment
is done
        result = (a%2==0) ? true :false;
        System.out.println("Result is -> " +
result);
    }
}
```

**Here is the output of above code.**

```
Result is -> true
Result is -> true
```

## 7.3 Switch statement

Switch statements are used to execute specific code block based upon the switch expression value.

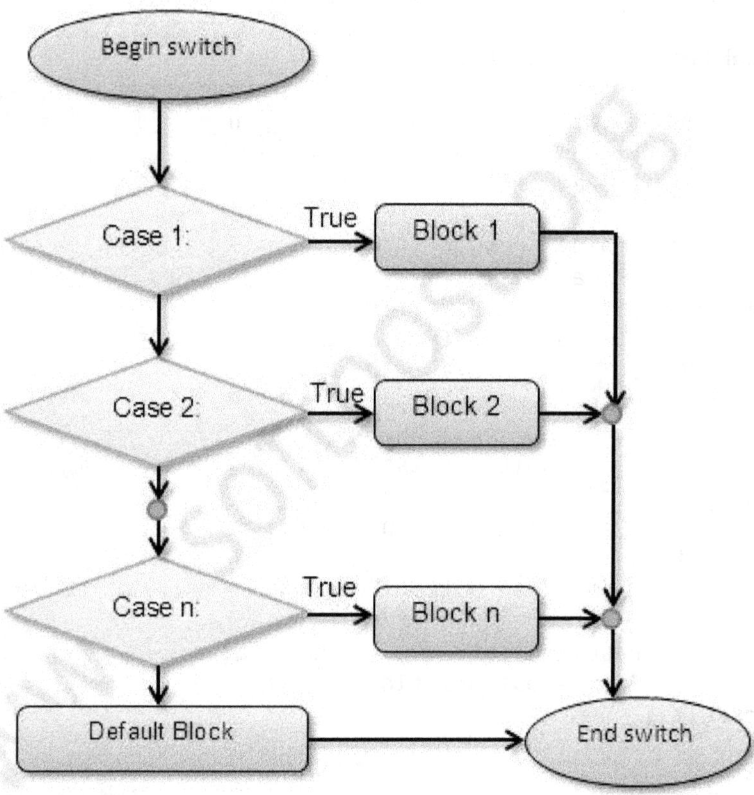


```
package Basicclass;
import java.io.*;
public class Basicjava
{
   public static void main(String[] args)
     {
       int a,b,c;
       int ch;
```

```
        BufferedReader br=new BufferedReader(new
InputStreamReader(System.in));
        try
        {
          System.out.println("Enter your hoice");
          ch=Integer.parseInt(br.readLine());

          System.out.println("Enter 1st Number");
          a=Integer.parseInt(br.readLine());

          System.out.println("Enter 2nd Number");
          b=Integer.parseInt(br.readLine());

// based on the value in ch, particular case block
is executed. If ch ==1, case 1 is called, if ch==2,
case 2 is called.

          switch(ch)
          {
           case 1:
               c=a+b;
               System.out.println("Addition is:"+c);
               break;
          case 2:
               c=a-b;
               System.out.println("Subtractionis:"+c);
               break;
          case 3:
               c=a*b;
            System.out.println("Multiplactionis:"+c);
               break;
          case 4:
               c=a/b;
               System.out.println("Dividation is:"+c);
               break;
          }
        }
        catch(Exception e)
        {}

        }
}
```

# 8. Loops in Java

There are 3 types of looping statements in Java.

1. while
2. do ....while
3. for – 2 variations and foreach method in Java 8 which is used to iterate through collection type of class

## 8.1 While Loop

Looping statements are used to repeat specific code.

```
package Basicclass;
import java.io.*;
public class Basicjava
 {
      public static void main(String[] args)
      {
            int i=1;
            try
            {
                  while(i<=10)
                  {
                        System.out.println(i);
                        i++;
                  }

            }
            catch(Exception e)
            {}

      }

}
```

## 8.2 do....while loop

do...while loop is similar to the while loop except one difference. Do...while block is executed at least once no matter what is the while condition.

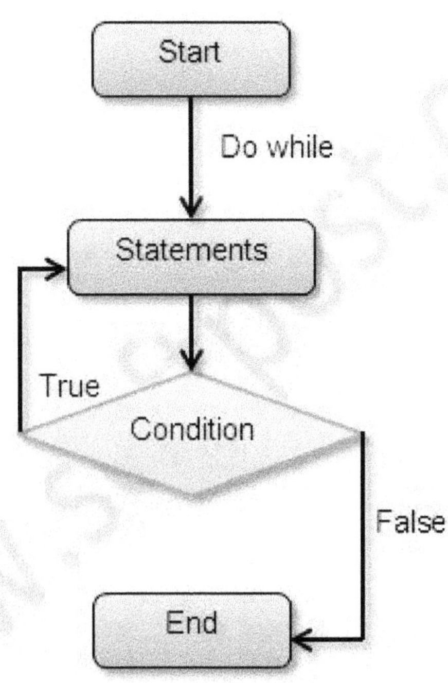


```
package Basicclass;
import java.io.*;
public class Basicjava {
	public static void main(String[] args)
	{
		int i=10;
		try
		{
			do
			{
				System.out.println(i);
				i++;
			}while(i<=20);
```

```
            }
            catch(Exception e)
            {}

    }
```

## 8.3 For Loop

for loop is preffered when you know exactly how many times you want to repeat the block of code.

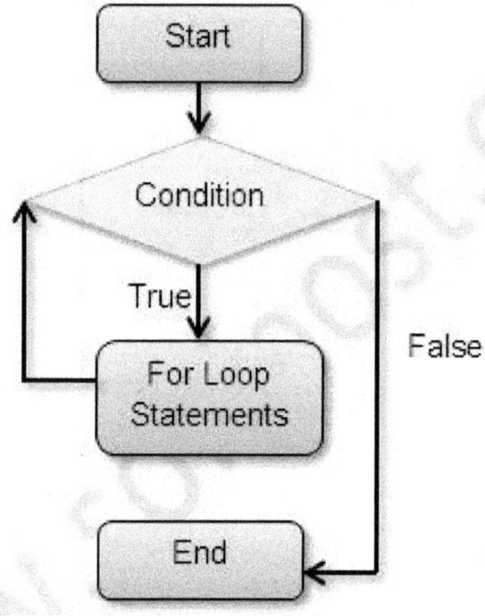


Below example will illustrate looping statements in Java.

```
package loops;
import java.util.ArrayList;

/**
 * Created by Sagar on 16-04-2016.
 */
```

```
public class Loops
{
    public static void main(String [] args)
    {
        //for loop
        for(int i=1;i<=3;i++)
         {
            System.out.println("Value of i in for
loop -> " + i);
         }
        //another for loop
        ArrayList<String> a = new ArrayList<>();
        a.add("Brisbane");
        a.add("Mumbai");
        a.add("London");
        for(String s : a)
        {
            //Print each element in ArrayList
            System.out.println("In other for loop ->
" + s);
        }

        //do loop
        int i = 1;
        do
        {
            System.out.println("Value of i in do
loop -> " + i++);
        }
        while(i<=4);

        //while loop
        i = 1;
        while(i<=4)
        {
            System.out.println("Value of i in While
loop -> " + i++);
        }

        //foreach using lambda expression
        a.forEach((s)->System.out.println("Inside
foreach loop -> " + s));
    }
}
```

**Here is the output of above Java example**

```
Value of i in for loop -> 1
Value of i in for loop -> 2
Value of i in for loop -> 3
In other for loop -> Brisbane
In other for loop -> Mumbai
In other for loop -> London
Value of i in do loop -> 1
Value of i in do loop -> 2
Value of i in do loop -> 3
Value of i in do loop -> 4
Value of i in While loop -> 1
Value of i in While loop -> 2
Value of i in While loop -> 3
Value of i in While loop -> 4
Inside foreach loop -> Brisbane
Inside foreach loop -> Mumbai
Inside foreach loop -> London
```

break and continue keyword in Java

break keyword is used to come out of loop. continue keyword is used to jump to next iteration in a loop. These keywords can be used in for loop, while loop, do…while loop

Below example illustrates the use of break and continue keywords.

```
package loops;
/**
 * Created by Sagar on 19-04-2016.
 */
public class BreakContinue
{
    public static void main(String [] args)
    {
        System.out.println("break keyword");
        //break keyword breaks out of loop and
executes next statement
        for (int i=1;i<10;i++)
        {
            if (i==5)
                break;
        System.out.println("value of i is -> " + i);
        }

        System.out.println("continue keyword");
        for (int i=1;i<10;i++)
        {
            //continue keyword takes control to the
beginning of loop
            //It does not execute statements that
follow
            if (i==5)
                continue;
        System.out.println("value of i is -> " + i);
        }

        int [] a = {1,2,3};
       for(int v:a)
        {
            System.out.println(v);
            break;
        }
    }
}
```

**Here is the output of above example.**

```
break keyword
value of i is -> 1
value of i is -> 2
value of i is -> 3
value of i is -> 4
continue keyword
value of i is -> 1
value of i is -> 2
value of i is -> 3
value of i is -> 4
value of i is -> 6
value of i is -> 7
value of i is -> 8
value of i is -> 9
1
```

```
package Basicclass;
import java.io.*;
public class Basicjava
 {
	public static void main(String[] args)
	{
		int i;
		String s="Welcome India";
		try
		{
```

```
            for(i=0;i<5;i++)
            {
                  System.out.println(s);
            }

            }
            catch(Exception e)
            {}
      }
}
```

# 9. Object oriented concepts in Java

Java is object oriented programming language.

Here is the list of various object oriented concepts in Java.

1. Class
2. Interface
3. Enum
4. Package
5. Inheritance
6. Encapsulation
7. Polymorphism
8. Abstraction

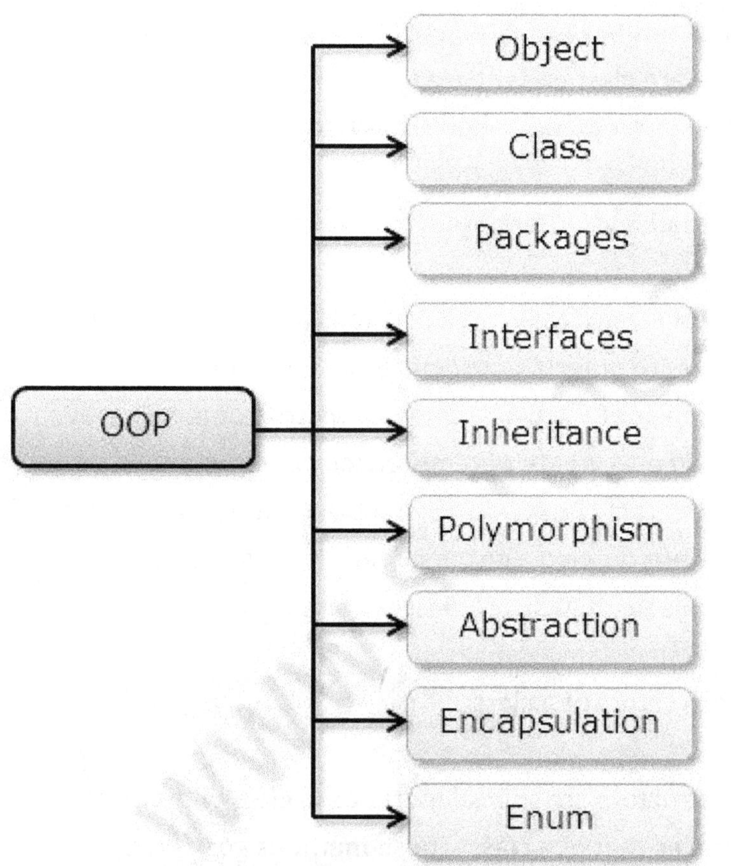


## 9.1 Classes in Java

In this topic, we will learn classes in Java.

A class is the kind of an entity in real world. Each class has certain attributes .

For example – Car, Student, Person, Phone, Account. All of these are classes. Each class has unique attributes (also called as members – fields/methods in Java).

At broad level, there are 2 types of classes.

1. Concrete classes – all methods are defined. We can create objects of concrete classes. When we create a object of the class, default constructor is called. We can also create parameterized constructors.
2. Abstract classes- In abstract class, at least one method is not defined. (just declared). We can not create objects of Abstract classes.

Constructors of a class

Constructors are special methods in class with the same name as that of a class. These methods get called automatically when we create an object of the class.

Here is an example of Concrete class.

```
package oops;

/**
 * Created by Sagar on 16-04-2016.
 */
public class Classes
 {
    public static void main(String [] args)
    {
        //Below statement creates the object
```

```
        Car audi = new Car();
        //accessing the method of the class Car
        audi.setMake("Audi");
        audi.setYear(2011);
        System.out.println("Audi is the Object of
type Car");
        //accessing the field of the class Car
        System.out.println("Year of audi car object
-> " + audi.year);
        //Another car object - Huyndai Santro
        Car i30 = new Car("Huyndai",2001);
        System.out.println("Year of i30 -> " +
i30.year);

    }
}

class Car
{
    //Each class has one or more Members (Fields and
Methods)
    //Fields of Class Car
    int year;
    String make;
    String model;
    //Constructors of Class
    //There can be one or more constructors
    //If you do not declare any constructor,
    //default empty constructor is used.
    Car()
    {
    System.out.println("Constructing empty object");
    }
    Car(String make, int year)
    {
       System.out.println("Constructing Car with
parameters");
       this.make = make;
       this.year = year;
    }

    //Methods of class
    public void setMake(String make)
{
```

```
        this.make = make;
    }
    public void setModel(String model)
    {
        this.model = model;
    }
    public void setYear(int year)
    {
        this.year = year;
    }
}
```

**Here is the output of above example.**

```
Constructing empty object
Audi is the Object of type Car
Year of audi car object -> 2011
Constructing Car with parameters
Year of i30 -> 2001
```

## 9.2 super keyword in Java

In this post, you will learn about super keyword in Java and how to use it to call super class constructors and methods.

In below example, Driver class extends Person class. From Driver class we have called the constructor and method of Person class using super keyword.

```
package inheritance;

/**
 * Created by ssalunke on 20/04/2016.
 */
public class SuperTest
{

    public static void main(String [] args)
    {
        Driver d = new Driver("Sagar","QLD-2627");
        d.displayName();
        d.displayDriverDetails();
    }

}

class Person
{
    String name;

    public Person(String name)
    {
        this.name = name;
        System.out.println("In Super class
constructor");
    }

    public void displayName()
    {
        System.out.println("In Super class.. Name is
-> " + this.name);
    }
}

class Driver extends Person
  {
    String regNo ;

    public Driver(String name, String reg)
     {
        //Invoke constructor of Super class
        super(name);
```

```
        this.regNo = reg;
        System.out.println("In Base class (Driver)
constructor");
    }

    public void displayDriverDetails()
    {
        //Invoke method from super class -
displayName
        super.displayName();
        System.out.println("In Base classs (Driver)
- regNo is -> "
                + this.regNo);
    }

}
```

**Here is the output of above Java example.**

```
In Super class constructor
In Base class (Driver) constructor
In Super class.. Name is -> Sagar
In Super class.. Name is -> Sagar
In Base classs (Driver) – regNo is -> QLD-2627
```

## 9.3 Interfaces in Java

Now let us try to understand interfaces in Java. Interfaces provide specification or standard. They tell what must be done. But they do not specify how it is to be done or implemented. Another class has to provide the implementation. Interfaces kind of create a standard set of methods as all classes implementing that interfaces must implement method with the same name.

Interfaces are like Classes in terms of syntax. Major difference between interfaces and classes are –

1. Interfaces contain only declaration of method. Concrete classes must have definitions of the methods. Abstract classes may contain undefined methods.
2. An interface can extend another interface (not a class) and can implement multiple interfaces. A class can implement multiple interfaces but can just extend one class.
3. All members of Interface are public by default.
4. Interfaces variables are final and static by default.
5. All methods of the Interface are abstract by default.

Example – In below example, we have a Movable interface with one method declaration move() and a variable MAX_SPEED. Class Bike implements that interface by providing definition of the method move().

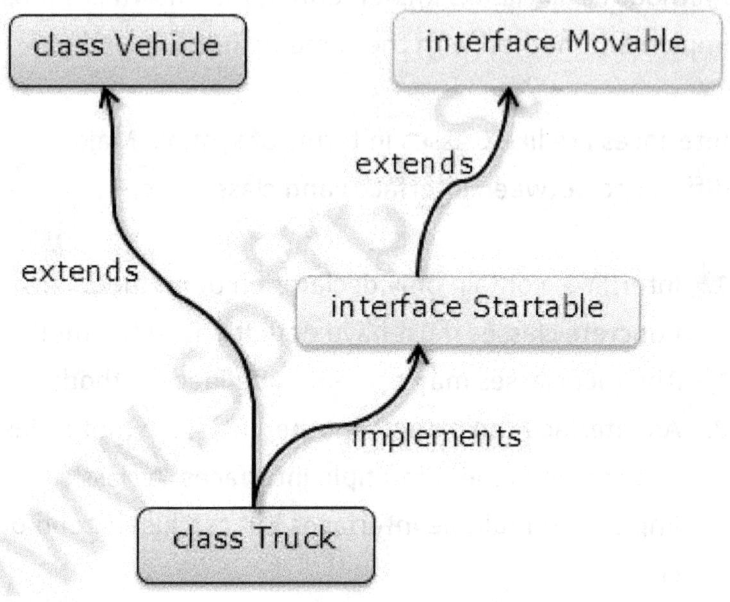


```
package oops;

/**
 * Created by Sagar on 16-04-2016.
 */
public class interface_implementation
{
    public static void main(String [] args)
    {
        Bike kawasaki = new Bike();
        kawasaki.move();
    }
}

class Bike implements Movable
{
    @Override
    public void move()
    {
        System.out.println("Move implementation");
        System.out.println("Max speed can be -> " +
Movable.MAX_SPEED);
```

```
    }
}

interface Movable
{
    int MAX_SPEED = 100;
    void move();
}
```

**Here is the output of Above Java example.**

```
Move implementation
Max speed can be -> 100
```

## 9.4 Enums in Java

It is like a class where we define constants. We can declare constants using final keyword but it is not meaningful. So we use enums. Enums are also type-safe. Another advantage of using Enum is that we can declare methods as well as constructors in Enum.

Below example demonstrates how we can use Enums in Java. We have created 2 Enums with names Coins and CoinsWithMethods. Since Enums are constant expressions, we can also use them in switch statement.

```
package enums;

/**
 * Created by ssalunke on 13/04/2016.
 */

public class TestEnums
{

    public static void main(String [] args)
    {

        Coins c = Coins.FIVE;

        //We can use enum in Switch statement as
shown in below code
        switch (c)
        {
            case ONE:
                System.out.println("You selected
Coin type - ONE");
                break;
            case FIVE:
                System.out.println("You selected
Coin type - FIVE");
                break;
            case TEN:
                System.out.println("You selected
Coin type - TEN");
                break;
        }

        CoinsWithMethods c1 = CoinsWithMethods.FIVE;

        //below line accesses the method of enum

        System.out.println("Year of Coin 5 is - > "
+ c1.getCoinYear());

  }

}
```

```
enum Coins
{
    ONE,
    FIVE,
    TEN
}

enum CoinsWithMethods
{
    ONE(2002),
    FIVE(2005),
    TEN(2007);

    private int coinYear;

    private CoinsWithMethods(int a)
    {
        coinYear = a;
    }

    int getCoinYear()
    {
        return this.coinYear;
    }

}
```

**Here is the output of above code.**

```
You selected Coin type – FIVE
Year of Coin 5 is – > 2005
```

## 9.5 Packages in Java

In this article, let us learn about packages in Java.

A package is nothing but a directory holding classes, interfaces and enums. All classes must be declared inside some package. If you do not specify the name of package, default package is used.

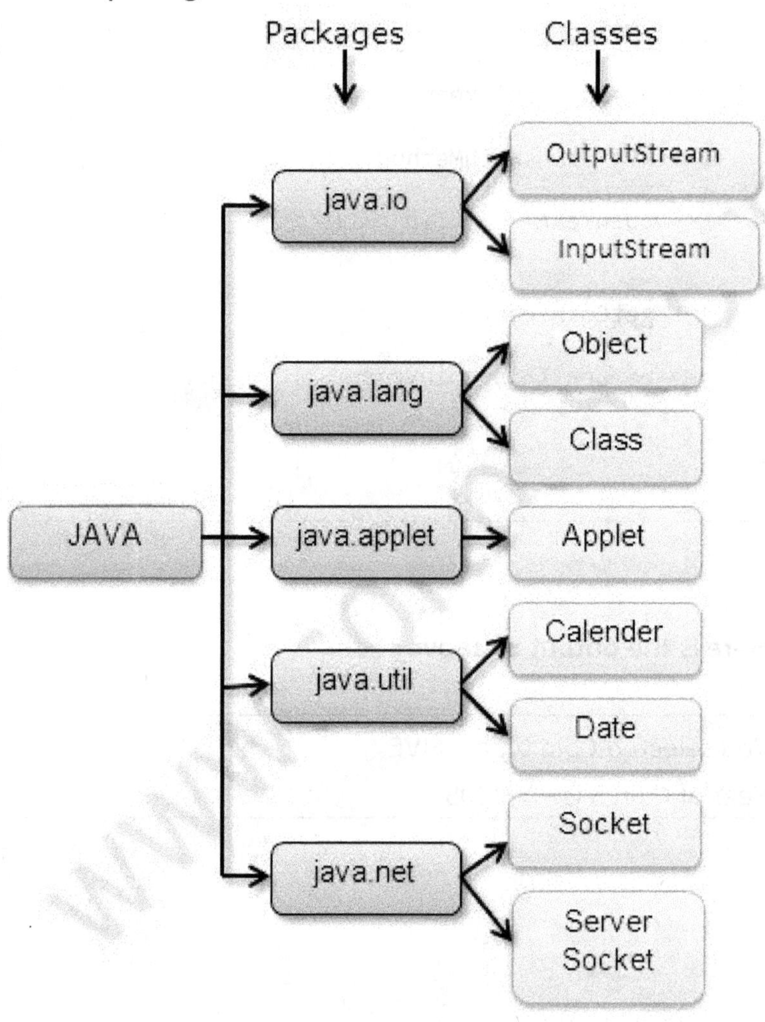

In below example, class Packages is inside oops package. Fully qualified name of the class is oops.Packages

```
//This class is in the package called as ooops
package oops;

//below statement will import all classes in java.io
package

import java.io.*;

//below statement will import only BigInteger class
in java.math package

import java.math.BigInteger;

public class Packages
{

    public static void main(String [] args)
    {
        BigInteger b = new BigInteger("8273892379");
        System.out.println("BigInteger -> " +
b.toString());

        System.out.println("File separator -> " +
File.pathSeparator);

    }
}
```

**Here is the output of above code –**

```
BigInteger -> 8273892379
File separator -> ;
```

## 9.6 static import in Java

To import specific member say class in a package in Java, we use below syntax.

```
import static java.io.File;
```

To import all members in a package in Java, we use below syntax.

```
import static java.io.*;
```

Both the statements above will import the **members in a package** like classes, interfaces etc.

With static import, it is possible to import the **static members of the class.**

For example – to import all static members in Math class, we can use below syntax.

```
import static java.lang.Math.*;
```

Below example explain how to use static import in Java.

```
package static_import;

import static java.lang.Math.*;

public class StaticImport
{
    public static void main(String [] args)
    {
```

```
        //Without static import, you will have to
use
        //Math.sqrt to invoke method.
        System.out.println("Square root of 625 is -
> " + sqrt(625));
    }
}
```

**Here is the output of above Java code.**

```
Square root of 625 is – > 25.0
```

## 9.7 Inheritance in Java

Now let us try to Inheritance in Java.

Inheritance allows child class to inherit the members of parent class. With inheritance concept, it is possible for one class to inherit the members of other class. Public and protected members of base class are inherited by child class.

Inheritance can be of 3 types in Java.

1. Single inheritance
2. Multi-level inheritance
3. Hierarchical inheritance

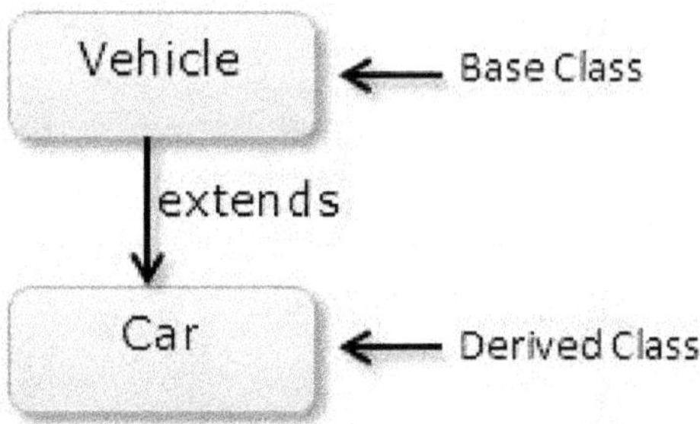
Single Inheritance
Vehicle
Base Class
extends
Car
Derived Class

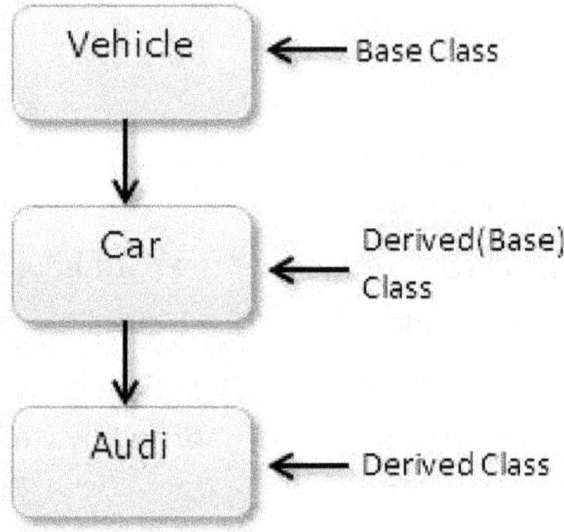
Multi Level Inheritance
Vehicle
Base Class
Car
Derived(Base) Class
Audi
Derived Class

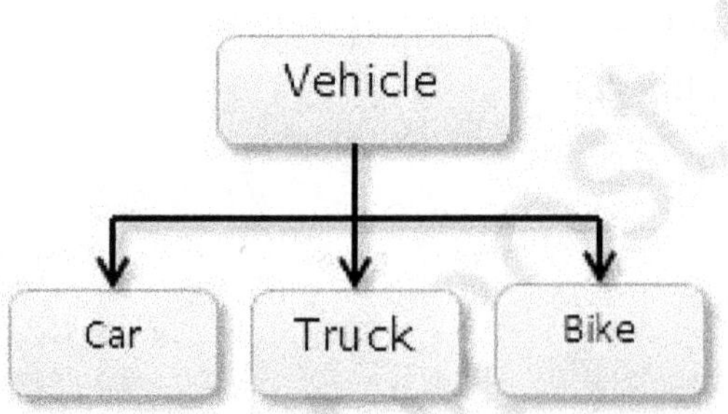
Hierarchical Inheritance
Vehicle
Car
Truck
Bike

Below example demonstrates all these concepts in detail.

```
package oops;

/**
 * Created by Sagar on 16-04-2016.
 */

public class ObjectOrientedClass
{
    public static void main(String [] args)
    {
        //Polymorphism can be of various type.
        //In below lines, we have used same Variable
v1
        // to refer to different types of objects
        Vehicle v1 = new Truck();
        System.out.println("Fule type of Truck -> "
+ v1.fuelType);
        v1.start();
        v1 = new MotorCycle();
        System.out.println("Fule type of MotorCycle
-> " + v1.fuelType);
        v1.start();

        //We can not access private members of any
class
        //This concept is called as Encapsulation.
        //v1.passengerCapacity is invalid. Outside
world does not know
        //what is going on inside a class.

        //Abstraction is achieved by using
interfaces or abstract methods.
        //Below example is valid.
        Startable s = new MotorCycle();
        //Below example will call MotorCycle's start
method.
        s.start();


    }
}
```

```
class Vehicle implements Startable
{
    protected String fuelType;
    public int year;
    public void start()
    {
        //System.out.println("Vehicle start");
    }
}

//By inheritance, Truck and MotorCycle class gets
protected
// and public members of parent class Vehicle

class Truck extends Vehicle
{
    private int GoodsCapacity;
    public Truck()
    {
        this.fuelType = "Diesel";
    }

    @Override
    public void start()
    {
        System.out.println("Truck start");
    }
}

class MotorCycle extends Vehicle
{
    private int passengerCapacity;
    public MotorCycle()
    {
        this.fuelType = "Petrol";
    }
    @Override
    public void start()
    {
        System.out.println("MotorCycle start");
    }
}
```

```
interface Startable
{
    void start();
}
```

**Here is the output of above example.**

```
Fule type of Truck -> Diesel
Truck start
Fule type of MotorCycle -> Petrol
MotorCycle start
MotorCycle start
```

## 9.8 Abstraction in Java

Abstraction means specifying only what has to be done but not how it has to be done.

We can achieve abstraction in Java by –

1. Interfaces
2. Abstract Classes

Below example explains how to use abstract classes in Java. In below example, Car is an abstract class.

```
package abstraction;
public class AbstractTest
{

    public static void main(String [] args)
    {
        //Below statement throws error saying Car is
abstract.. can not instantiate
        //Car c = new Car()

        //Below statement will work..
        HatchbackCar c1 = new HatchbackCar();
        c1.move();

    }
}

abstract class Car
{
    public abstract void move();
}

class HatchbackCar extends Car
{
    public void move()
    {
        System.out.println("Hatchback move method");
    }
}
```

**Here is the output of above code.**

```
Hatchback move method
```

## 9.9 Encapsulation in Java

Encapsulation means hiding the implementation details from the outside world.

Encapsulation means hiding the implementation details from the outside world.

Below image shows how encapsulation is achieved in Java by declaring the private members of the class. Remember that We can not access the private members from outside of the class. Thus, any changes made inside the class with respect to private members do not impact outside classes.

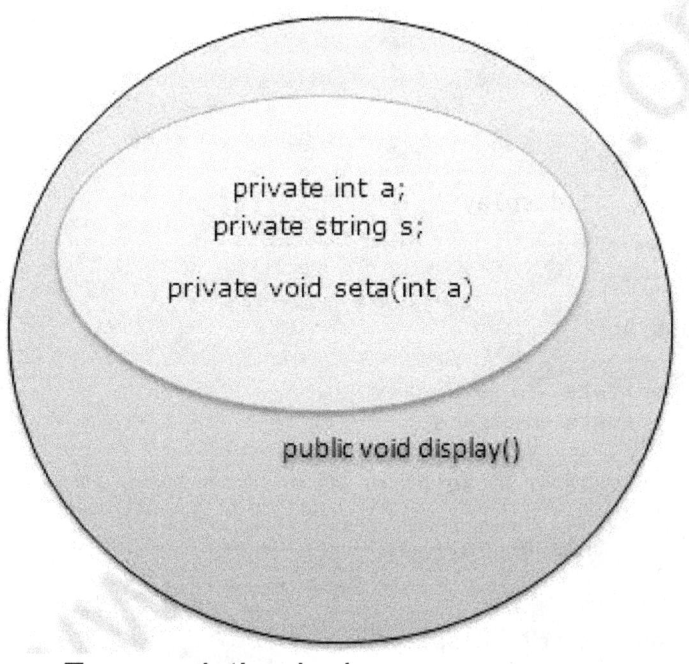
private int a;
private string s;
private void seta(int a)
public void display()

Encapsulation in Java

Below example illustrates how encapsulation works in Java.

```
package encapsulation;

/**
 * Created by ssalunke on 19/04/2016.
 */
public class Encapsulation
{
    public static void main(String [] args)
    {
        A a1 = new A();

        //We can not access private members from
here
        //Below line will throw compilation error
saying a has private access
        //a1.a
        //Below line will throw compilation error
saying seta has private access
        //a1.seta(1)

        //We can access public members from outside
of class
        a1.display();
    }
}

class A
{
    private int a;
    private String s;

    private void seta(int a)
    {
        this.a = a;
    }

    public void display()
    {
        System.out.println("Display");
    }
}
```

**Here is the output of above code.**

```
Display
```

## 9.10 Polymorphism in Java

Polymorphism means one name but many forms. In Java, we can achieve Polymorphism by method overloading and overriding.

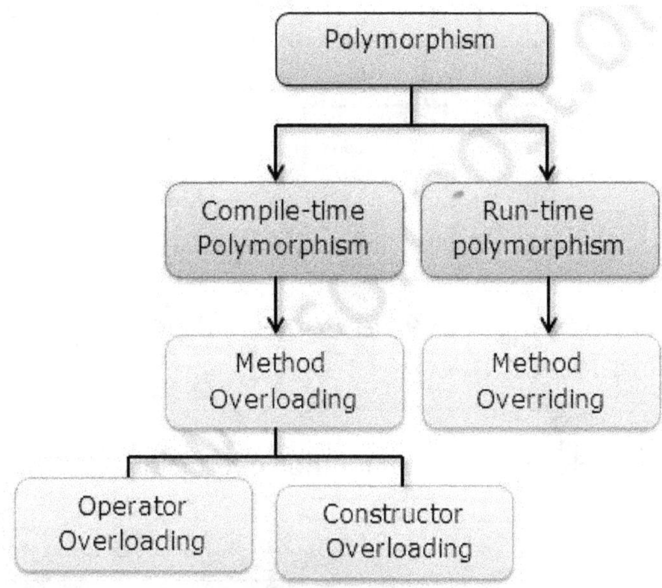


*Types of Polymorphism*

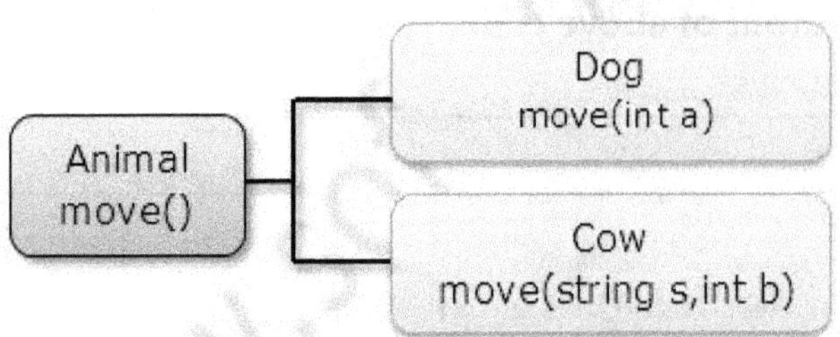


*Method Overloading (Same name, different parameters)*

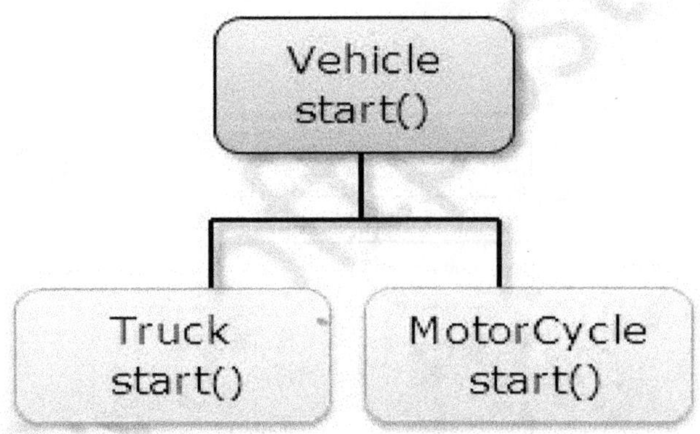


*Overriding - (Same name, different implementation)*

Below example explains how method overloading and overriding works in Java.

```
package polymorphism;

/**
 * Created by ssalunke on 19/04/2016.
 */
public class Polymorphism {

    public static void main(String [] args)
{
```

```
        //method overloading - Same method name but
different arguments
        String city = "Bali";
        System.out.println(city.substring(0));
        System.out.println(city.substring(0, 3));

        //Method overriding
        Polymorphism p = new Polymorphism();

        //toString method is already defined in
java.lang.Object class
        //But we have over-ridden that method in
class Polymorphism

        System.out.println(p.toString());

    }

    @Override
    public String toString()
    {
        return "Polymorphism - " + this.hashCode();
    }
}
```

**Here is the output of above code.**

```
Bali
Bal
Polymorphism - 999966131
```

# 10. Characters

Below example will illustrate various ways in which we can create a character and perform operations on it.

```
package strings;

public class CharacterClass
{

    public static void main(String [] args)
    {
        char c1 = 'a';

        //check if c1 is lower case
        System.out.println("Is c1 lower case -? -> "
+ Character.isLowerCase(c1));

        //check if c1 is upper case
        System.out.println("Is c1 upper case -? -> "
+ Character.isUpperCase(c1));

        //check if c1 is a white space
        System.out.println("Is c1 a white space ? ->
" + Character.isWhitespace(c1));

        //check if c1 is a digit
        System.out.println("Is c1 digit? -> " +
Character.isDigit(c1));

        //check if c1 is a letter
        Character c2 = '$';
        System.out.println("Is c2($) letter? -> " +
Character.isLetter(c2));

        //check if c1 is a alphabetic
        System.out.println("Is c2($) alphabetic? ->
" + Character.isAlphabetic(c2));

    }
}
```

**Here is the output of above program.**

```
Is c1 lower case -? -> true
Is c1 upper case -? -> false
Is c1 a white space ? -> false
Is c1 digit? -> false
Is c2($) letter? -> false
Is c2($) alphabetic? -> false
```

# 11. Boxing and Unboxing in Java

Collections in Java does not support primitives. We can not store primitives in collection objects. Only objects can be stored in collections.

Below statement is invalid.

```
//ArrayList<int> list = new ArrayList<>();
```

But still we can store integers in ArrayList using a concept called as Boxing. Process by which primitives like int are converted into objects of Wrapper classes like Integer, Double etc is called as Boxing. The reverse process is called as Unboxing.

Below example illustrates Boxing and Unboxing in Java.

```
package boxing;

import java.util.ArrayList;

/**
 * Created by ssalunke on 19/04/2016.
 */
public class Boxing
{

    public static void main(String args [])
     {

        //Below statement is invalid
        //ArrayList<int> list = new ArrayList<>();

        int c = 3;
```

```
        ArrayList<Integer> list = new ArrayList<>();
        list.add(2); //boxing to Integer wrapper
        list.add(c); //boxing to Integer wrapper

        //Unboxing occurs when storing integer
object to primitive type

        int a = list.get(0);
        System.out.println("First value in list is "
+ a);

    }
}
```

**Here is the output of above example.**

```
First value in list is 2
```

# 12. Number conversion and casting in Java

## 12.1 Typecasting

We can convert the data types using wrapper classes like Integer, Boolean etc.

There are 2 types of casting.

1. Implicit
2. Explicit

In implicit type of conversion, data type of the variable is automatically converted to another data type with higher size.

Implicit Data Type Conversion example –

```
int x = 11; // occupies 4 bytes
double y = x; // occupies 8 bytes
System.out.println(y);
// prints 11.0
```

Explicit Data Type Conversion example –

As shown in below example, we have converted the data type of x (double) to int.

```
double x = 11.5;
int y = (int) x;
```

We can also convert the object of one type to another using casting.

Please note that sub-class to parent class casting is implicit. But Parent class to sub class casting has to be done explicitly.

In this post, let us learn how to convert the strings to numbers like int, float, double and vice versa. We will also learn how to convert the int, float, double to each other.

Below example will illustrate how to convert and type cast the numbers in Java.

```
package numbers;

/**
 * Created by ssalunke on 14/04/2016.
 */
public class NumberConversionCasting
{
    public static void main(String [] args) throws
Exception
    {

        System.out.println(new
Double("120.11").doubleValue());

        //Converting String to integer
```

```
        String amount = "2323";
        System.out.println("String converted into
int -> "
                + Integer.parseInt(amount));

        //Converting String to double
        amount = "232323.4545";
        System.out.println("String converted into
double -> "
                + Double.parseDouble(amount));

        //Converting String to double
        double cost = 232323.4545;
        System.out.println("double converted into
string -> "
                + String.valueOf(cost) instanceof
String);

    //Converting string containing $ to pure number.
    // Remove all special characters before
        amount = "$87282.38";
        amount = amount.replaceAll("\\$","");
      System.out.println("After replacing the $ -> "
                + Double.valueOf(amount));

        //converting the number to string
        double d = 78287.22;
        System.out.println("String representation of
double is -> "+ String.valueOf(d));

        //casting double to int
        int x = (int) d;
        System.out.println("After casting double to
integer -> " + x);

    }
}
```

**Here is the output of above program.**

```
120.11
String converted into int -> 2323
String converted into double -> 232323.4545
true
After replacing the $ -> 87282.38
String representation of double is -> 78287.22
After casting double to integer -> 78287
```

## 12.2 Formatting numbers in Java

In this post, we will learn how to to format numbers in Java.

Some times we need to format the number as per locale or as per our custom requirement. We also have a requirement to round the numbers. That's when Formatting classes can help you.

There are 2 important classes - NumberFormat and DecimalFormat to format numbers in Java.

```
package numbers;

import java.math.BigDecimal;
import java.text.DecimalFormat;
import java.text.NumberFormat;
import java.util.Currency;
import java.util.Locale;
```

```
/**
 * Created by ssalunke on 14/04/2016.
 */
public class NumberFormatting
{

    public static void main(String [] args) throws
Exception
     {

        //Converting number to local geographical
representation
        System.out.println("Number 564656 as in
Germany -> "
                +
NumberFormat.getNumberInstance(Locale.GERMANY).forma
t(564656));

        System.out.println("Number 564656 as in
France -> "
                +
NumberFormat.getNumberInstance(Locale.FRANCE).format
(564656));

        System.out.println("Number 564656 as in US -
> " +

NumberFormat.getNumberInstance(Locale.US).format(564
656));


        //Adding $ to beginning of string
        NumberFormat numberFormat =
NumberFormat.getCurrencyInstance(new Locale("En",
"US"));
        String currencyString =
numberFormat.format(120.99);
        System.out.println(currencyString);

        //Stripping $ from the string
        Number n = numberFormat.parse("$120");
        System.out.println("Number -> " +
n.doubleValue());
```

```
        //Rounding the numbers
        double decimal = 6.3267;
        DecimalFormat decimalFormat = new
DecimalFormat("#.00");
        System.out.println("After rounding the
number to 2 decimal -> "+
Double.valueOf(decimalFormat.format(decimal)));

    }
}
```

**Here is the output of above code.**

```
Number 564656 as in Germany -> 564.656
Number 564656 as in France -> 564 656
Number 564656 as in US -> 564,656
$120.99
Number -> 120.0
After rounding the number to 2 decimal -> 6.33
```

# 13. Arrays

Arrays are used to store similar types of elements in sequential manner. Arrays are fixed in size. You can not grow or shrink the size of array once initialized.

Example -

```
int [] a = {11,22,33}
Student [] studentArray = {s1,s2,s3}
```

There are 3 types of arrays in Java.

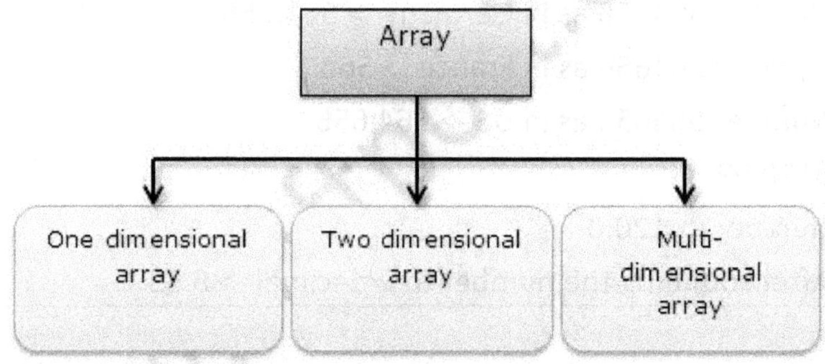


1. Single Dimensional
2. 2-Dimensional
3. Multi-dimensional

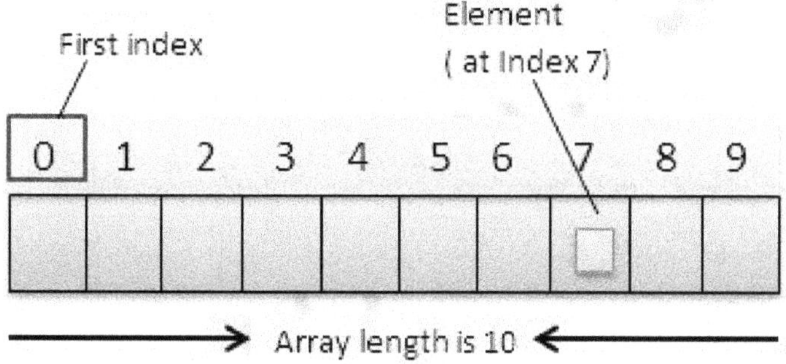


*Single dimensional Array*

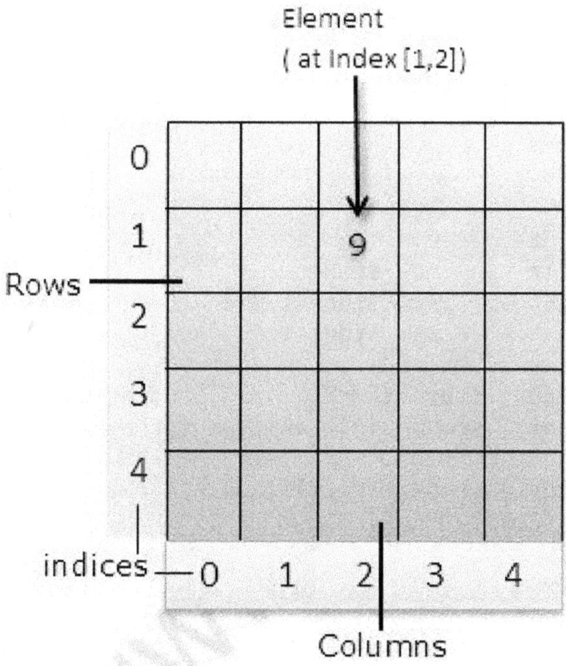


*2 dimensional Array*

Below example explains how to use arrays in Java.

```
package arrays;

/**
 * Created by ssalunke on 18/04/2016.
 */
public class Array
{

    public static void main(String [] args)
    {

        System.out.println("Let us learn One
dimensional array");

        int[] primitiveIntArray = new int[3];
        int[] primitiveInitializedIntArray =
{1,2,3};
        int[] primitiveInitializedIntArray1 = new
int[]{1,2,3};

        //Just like primitives, we can store the
reference
        // types of objects in Arrays
        Student s1 = new Student("s1");
        Student s2 = new Student("s2");
        Student s3 = new Student("s3");

        Student[] studentArray = new Student[3];
        Student[] studentInitializedIntArray =
{s1,s2,s3};
        Student[] studentInitializedIntArray1 = new
Student[]{s1,s2,s3};

        //Accessing elements in array by using for
loop
        for(int i=0;i<=2;i++){
            System.out.println("Integer Array -> "
                    +
primitiveInitializedIntArray[i]);
            System.out.println("Student Array -> "
                    +
studentInitializedIntArray[i]);

    }
```

```
        //Accessing elements in array using another
variation of for loop

      for(int e: primitiveInitializedIntArray)
      {
       System.out.println("Integer Array -> " + e );
      }

      for(Student e: studentInitializedIntArray)
      {
       System.out.println("Student Array -> " + e );
      }


//**************************************************
************//
        //Learning 2 dimensional arrays

    int [][] twoDimensionalIntArray = new int[3][3];
        for(int i=0;i<=2;i++)
            for(int j=0;j<=2;j++)
            {
                twoDimensionalIntArray[i][j] = i+j;
            }

        for(int[] e: twoDimensionalIntArray)
        {
            for(int j:e)
                System.out.println("2-D Integer
Array -> " + j);
        }

        //Array of Arrays in Java
        int[][] intArrayOfArray =
{primitiveInitializedIntArray,primitiveInitializedIn
tArray1};

        int[][][] intArrayOf2DArray =
{twoDimensionalIntArray,twoDimensionalIntArray};

        System.out.println("1st Element in
intArrayOfArray -> "+ intArrayOfArray[0][0]);
```

```
        System.out.println("1st Element in
intArrayOf2DArray -> "+ intArrayOf2DArray[0][0][0]);

    }

}

class Student
{
    String name;

    Student(String s)
    {
        this.name = s;
    }

    @Override
    public String toString()
    {
        return this.name;
    }
}
```

**Here is the output of above code.**

```
Let us learn One dimensional array
Integer Array -> 1
Student Array -> s1
Integer Array -> 2
Student Array -> s2
Integer Array -> 3
Student Array -> s3
Integer Array -> 1
Integer Array -> 2
```

```
Integer Array -> 3
Student Array -> s1
Student Array -> s2
Student Array -> s3
2-D Integer Array -> 0
2-D Integer Array -> 1
2-D Integer Array -> 2
2-D Integer Array -> 1
2-D Integer Array -> 2
2-D Integer Array -> 3
2-D Integer Array -> 2
2-D Integer Array -> 3
2-D Integer Array -> 4
1st Element in intArrayOfArray -> 1
1st Element in intArrayOf2DArray -> 0
```

## 14. Command line arguments in java

We can pass the input arguments to the Java program through command line. main() method accepts those arguments in the form of string array.

Below example explains how we can use command line arguments in Java.

```
package commandline;

/**
 * Created by ssalunke on 20/04/2016.
 */
public class CommandLine
{

    public static void main(String [] args)
    {

        //javac commandline/CommandLine.java
        //java -cp . commandline.CommandLine sagar
salunke
        System.out.println("Total number of
arguments -> " + args.length);
        System.out.println("value of first argument
-> " + args[0]);
        System.out.println("value of second argument
-> " + args[1]);

    }
}
```

**Here is the output of above Java example.**

```
Total number of arguments -> 2
value of first argument -> Sagar
value of second argument -> Salunke
```

# 15. Variable Number of arguments in Java

Before Java 5.0, all methods could have fixed number of arguments.

In Java 5.0, Sun introduced variable number of arguments concept. With variable number of arguments, you can pass any number of arguments to same method. You do not need to create a separate method.

Below example explains how to use variable number of arguments in Java. Note that we have used data type as int...

... indicate that there will be variable number of arguments. Arguments are passed as an array and can be retrieved using array syntax.

```
package other;

/**
 * Created by Sagar on 20-04-2016.
 */

public class VarArgs
{

    public static void main(String [] args)
    {
        add(2,3);
        add(4,5,6);
        add(7,8,9,10,11,12);
    }
```

```
    public static void add(int... arg)
    {
        System.out.println("Total number of
arguments -> " + arg.length);
        int sum = 0;
        for(int a : arg)
        {
            sum += a;
        }

        System.out.println("Sum of numbers is -> " +
sum);
    }
}
```

**Here is the output of above Java Example.**

```
Total number of arguments -> 2
Sum of numbers is -> 5
Total number of arguments -> 3
Sum of numbers is -> 15
Total number of arguments -> 6
Sum of numbers is -> 57
```

# 16. Exception handling in Java

Exception is an unexpected event that might occur at the time of executing the program. For example - if you are trying to open a file with name xyz.txt and that file does not exist on disk. At that time, you will get Exception viz. FileNotFoundException

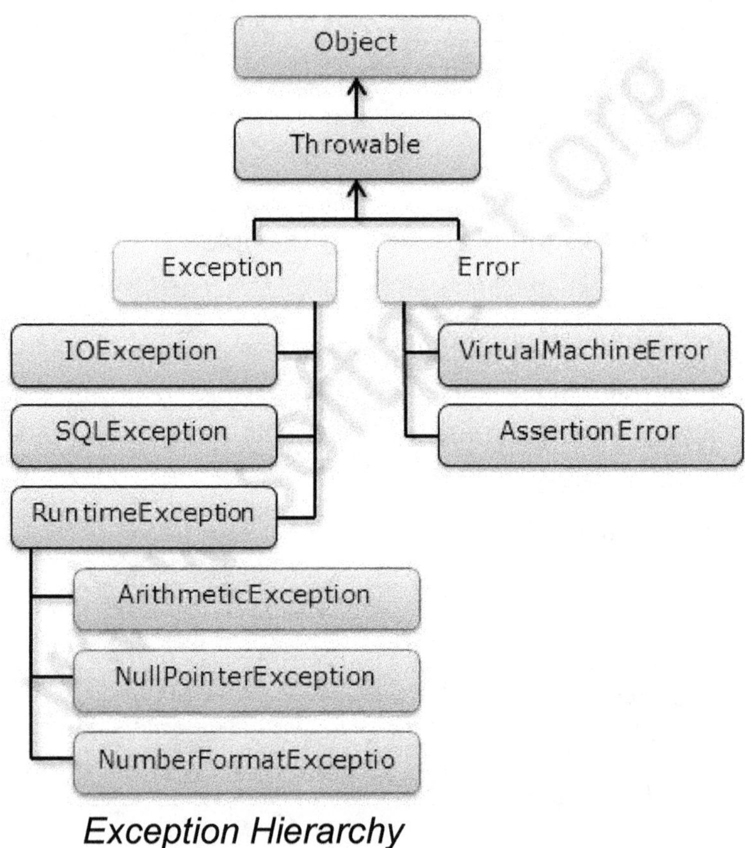


*Exception Hierarchy*

So if you think some part of code is risky and might throw Exception, you need to handle it so that program will continue to run in graceful manner.

In Java, we can use try.....catch construct to handle the Exceptions.

There are 2 types of Exceptions in Java.

1. Checked Exception
2. Unchecked Exception

Your code will not compile unless you handle checked exception. Unchecked exception happen at run time. For example - divide by zero exception.

**throw and throws keyword in Java**

throw keyword is used to throw custom exception. throws keyword is used when you do not want to handle the exception in current method. In this case, the caller of the method will have to handle the exception.

Below example illustrates how we can use try ....catch to handle exception.

```
package exceptions;

import org.testng.reporters.Files;
import java.io.File;
import java.io.FileNotFoundException;
import java.io.IOException;

/**
 * Created by Sagar on 16-04-2016.
 */
public class TestExceptions
{
    public static void main(String [] args)
    {
        try
        {
            Files.writeFile("shs",new
File("c:\\xx"));
        }
        catch (FileNotFoundException ex)
        {
            System.out.println("File not found
Exception occured");
            ex.printStackTrace();
        }
        catch (IOException ex)
        {
            ex.printStackTrace();
        }
        finally
        {
            System.out.println("This finally block
of code will be executed"+ " No matter if Exception
is thrown or not");
        }

        System.out.println("Program continuing even
after Exception comes");

        //Unchecked Exception - ArithmeticException
        //If you comment below line, program will
exit with code 0
```

```
        System.out.println("this line throws"+11/0);

    }
}
```

**Here is the sample output of above example**

```
This finally block of code will be executed No
matter if Exception is thrown or not
Program continuing even after Exception comes

Process finished with exit code 1
File not found Exception occured
java.io.FileNotFoundException: c:\xx (Access is
denied)
Exception in thread "main"
java.lang.ArithmeticException: / by zero
This finally block of code will be executed No
matter
if Exception is thrown or not
Program continuing even after Exception comes
```

# 17. String handling in Java

## 17.1 String class

String is nothing but a sequence of characters. Various ways in which you can create strings in Java are given below.

1. char [] city = {'B','r','i','s','b','a','n','e'}
2. String city = "Brisbane"
3. String city = new String(city)
4. String city = new String("Brisbane")
5. StringBuffer city = new StringBuffer("Brisbane")
6. StringBuilder city = new StringBuilder("Brisbane")

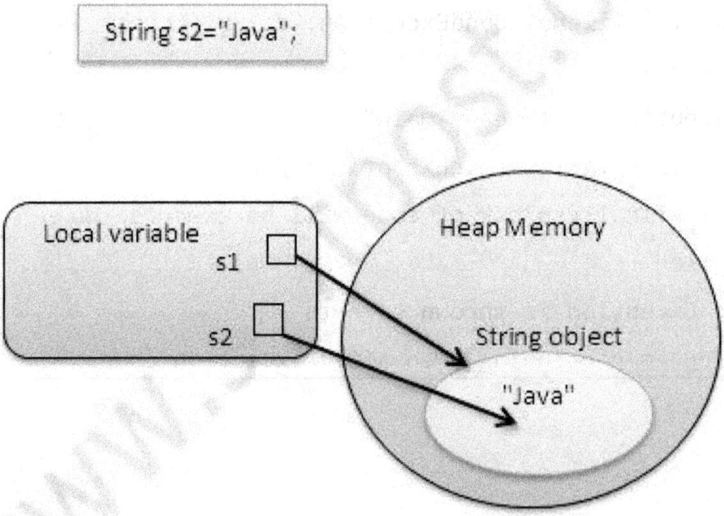

There are 2 types of strings in Java.

1. Immutable – Strings created in examples 1 – 4 are immutable strings
2. Mutable - StringBuffer and StringBuilder. When you think that strings are going to modified many times, you can use these classes. Difference between StringBuffer and StringBuilder is that StringBuffer is synchronized while StringBuilder is not.

Below Java example illustrates all important methods of String class.

```
package strings;

/**
 * Created by Sagar on 16-04-2016.
 */
public class strings
{

    public static void main(String [] args)
    {
        String city = new String("Brisbane");
        System.out.println("String in focus -> " +
city);

        //To get the character at specific index

        System.out.println("Character at index 0 ->
" + city.charAt(0));

        //To get the ascii value of a character at
specific index
```

```
        System.out.println("Ascii value of Character
at index 0 -> " + city.codePointAt(0));

       //To compare the strings
lexicographically/alphabetically

        System.out.println("Comparing Brisbane with
Sydney lexicographically -> " +
city.compareTo("Sydney"));

        System.out.println("Comparing Brisbane with
Sydney in case insensitive manner -> " +
city.compareToIgnoreCase("Sydney"));

        //To concatinate the string
        System.out.println("Concatinating Sydney to
Brisbane -> " + city.concat("Sydney"));

        System.out.println("city is still pointing
to Brisbane -> " + city);

        //To check if String contains other string

        System.out.println("Brisbane contains bane?
-> " + city.contains("bane"));

        //To check if string1's content is equal to
string 2

        System.out.println("is Brisbane equal to
Sydney? -> " + city.contentEquals("Sydney"));

        System.out.println("is Brisbane equal to
Brisbane? -> " + city.contentEquals("Brisbane"));

        //To check if String ends with other string

        System.out.println("Brisbane ends with bane?
-> " + city.endsWith("bane"));

        //To check if String starts with other
string
        System.out.println("Brisbane starts with
bane? -> " + city.startsWith("bane"));
```

```
        //To check if String matches with other
string in case insensitive manner

        System.out.println("Brisbane is equals to
Sydney? -> " + city.equalsIgnoreCase("Sydney"));

        //To check if String variable is empty

        System.out.println("Brisbane is empty? -> "
+ city.isEmpty());

        //To get the length of the string

        System.out.println("Brisbane length is -> "
+ city.length());

        //replace - to replace the character in
string by other character

        System.out.println("Replacing B by C -> " +
city.replace('B','C'));

        //replaceAll - to replace the pattern in
string with other string

        System.out.println("Replacing B by C -> " +
city.replaceAll("B","C"));

        System.out.println("Replacing [Bb] by C -> "
+ city.replaceAll("[Bb]","C"));

        //matches - to check if string matches with
the pattern as it is

        System.out.println("Brisbane matches with
Brisbane? -> " + city.matches("Brisbane"));

        //split - to split the string by delimiter

        System.out.println("Splitting Brisbane by s
-> " + city.split("s")[0]);
```

```
        System.out.println("Splitting Brisbane by s
-> " + city.split("s")[1]);

        //substring - to get the substring from
original string

        System.out.println("Substring of Brisbane in
the range 4-8 -> " + city.substring(4,8));

        //toCharArray - to convert the string into
array
        char [] array = city.toCharArray();
        System.out.println("Brisbane in array -> " +
array[0] + array[1] + array[2]);

        //toLowerCase - to convert the string to
lower case

        System.out.println("Brisbane in lower case
is -> " + city.toLowerCase());

        //toUpperCase - to convert the string to
upper case

        System.out.println("Brisbane in upper case
is -> " + city.toUpperCase());

        //trim - to remove the white spaces from
start and end of the string

        System.out.println("Brisbane after trimming
is -> " + city.trim());

    }
}
```

**Here is the output of above Java example**

```
String in focus -> Brisbane

Character at index 0 -> B
```

```
Ascii value of Character at index 0 -> 66
Comparing Brisbane with Sydney lexicographically ->
-17
Comparing Brisbane with Sydney in case insensitive
manner -> -17
Concatinating Sydney to Brisbane -> BrisbaneSydney
city is still pointing to Brisbane -> Brisbane
Brisbane contains bane? -> true
is Brisbane equal to Sydney? -> false
is Brisbane equal to Brisbane? -> true
Brisbane ends with bane? -> true
Brisbane starts with bane? -> false
Brisbane is equals to Sydney? -> false
Brisbane is empty? -> false
Brisbane length is -> 8
Replacing B by C -> Crisbane
Replacing B by C -> Crisbane
Replacing [Bb] by C -> CrisCane
Brisbane matches with Brisbane? -> true
Splitting Brisbane by s -> Bri
Splitting Brisbane by s -> bane
Substring of Brisbane in the range 4-8 -> bane
Brisbane in array -> Bri
Brisbane in lower case is -> brisbane
Brisbane in upper case is -> BRISBANE
Brisbane after trimming is -> Brisbane
```

## 17.2 StringBuffer and StringBuilder in Java

As you know, String objects are immutable. Every time you create a String object, you can not change it at all. So if you create 1 string object and appended something into it, a new String object is created altogether. This wastes the memory.

That's when StringBuffer and StringBuilder comes into picture. Objects of StringBuffer and StringBuilder classes are mutable. StringBuffer and StringBuilder are also better than String as compared to performance.

**Difference between StringBuffer and StringBuilder**

So both StringBuffer and StringBuilder are mutable. Which one should you use? Difference between StringBuffer and StringBuilder is that StringBuffer is synchronized while StringBuilder is not. So when you want thread-safety, you should go ahead with StrignBuffer otherwise you should go ahead with StringBuilder.

Below example illustrates how to use StringBuilder and StringBuffer in Java.

```
package strings;

/**
 * Created by Sagar on 20-04-2016.
 */
public class StringBuilderBuffer
{

    public static void main(String [] args)
    {

        //StringBuffer should be used when you want
thread safety
        StringBuffer stringBuffer = new
StringBuffer("softpost");

        stringBuffer.append(".org");
        System.out.println("Using StringBuffer -> "
+ stringBuffer);

        //StringBuilder should be used when you are
using single thread

        StringBuilder stringBuilder = new
StringBuilder("Sagar");

        stringBuilder.append("Salunke");

        System.out.println("Using StringBuilder -> "
+stringBuilder);
    }
}
```

**Here is the output of above code.**

```
Using StringBuffer -> softpost.org
Using StringBuilder -> SagarSalunke
```

# 18. Mathematical Operations in Java

In this post, we will learn how to perform mathematical operations on numbers – power, squre root, floor, ceil, rounding numbers

Here is the program that illustrates various mathematical operations in Java.

```
package numbers;

/**
 * Created by ssalunke on 14/04/2016.
 */
public class Maths
{

    public static void main(String [] args) throws
Exception
    {

        //Get absolute value
        System.out.println("Absolute value of -
2929.2 -> " + Math.abs(-2929.2));

        //Rounding to 0 decimals
        System.out.println("Round of the number -
234.221 is ->" +" " + Math.round(-234.221));

        //Power method
        System.out.println("2^3 is -> " +
Math.pow(2, 3));

        //Finding square root
        System.out.println("Square root of 525 -> "
+ Math.sqrt(525));
```

```
        //Get random value
        System.out.println("Random number -> " +
String.valueOf(Math.random()));

    }
}
```

**Here is the output of mathematical operations.**

```
Absolute value of -2929.2 -> 2929.2
Round of the number -234.221 is -> -234
2^3 is -> 8.0
Square root of 525 -> 22.9128784747792
Random number -> 0.6005728946831648
```

# 19. Date and Time in Java

In this post, you will learn how to handle date and time in Java.

3 important classes to work with Date and time in Java are

1. Date - Legacy date class.
2. Calendar - calculating the difference between dates, adding, deleting duration from dates.
3. SimpleDateFormat - formatting dates.

Below example illustrates how we can use Date, Calendar and SimpleDateFormat classes in Java.

```
package datetime;

import java.text.*;
import java.util.*;

public class DateTime
{
    public static void main(String[] args) throws
Exception
     {

        //SimpleDateFormat can be used to specify
the format of date
        //example - yyyy/MM/dd HH:mm:ss, MM/dd/yyyy

        DateFormat dateFormat = new
SimpleDateFormat("dd-MM-yyyy");

        Calendar cal = Calendar.getInstance();

        System.out.println("Todays date -> "
```

```
                + dateFormat.format(cal.getTime()));

        //get future date by adding 15 days to
current date

        cal.add(Calendar.DATE, 15);
        System.out.println("15 Days from today -> "
                + dateFormat.format(cal.getTime()));

        //get past date by subtracting 25 days from
it.
        cal.add(Calendar.DATE, -25);
        System.out.println("25 days in the past -> "
                + dateFormat.format(cal.getTime()));

        //For comparing dates, use Date class

        Date date1 = dateFormat.parse("11-12-2020");
        Date date2 = dateFormat.parse("11-12-2016");
        Date date3 = new Date();

        System.out.println("date 1 -> " +
dateFormat.format(date1));

        System.out.println("date 2 -> " +
dateFormat.format(date2));

        System.out.println("date 3 -> " +
dateFormat.format(date3));

        if (date1.before(date2))
            System.out.println("Date1 falls before
Date2");

        if (date1.after(date3))
            System.out.println("Date1 falls after
Date3");

        if (date1.equals(date2))
            System.out.println("Date1 and Date2 fall
on same day");

    }
}
```

**Here is the output of above Java example**

```
Todays date -> 16-04-2016
15 Days from today -> 01-05-2016
25 days in the past -> 06-04-2016
date 1 -> 11-12-2020
date 2 -> 11-12-2016
date 3 -> 16-04-2016
Date1 falls after Date3
```

# 20. Regular expressions in Java

Regular expressions are used to check if the text contains specific pattern (Regular Expression).

There are 2 most important classes that support regular expressions in Java.

1. Pattern
2. Matcher

```
package regular_expressions;

import java.util.regex.Matcher;
import java.util.regex.Pattern;

/**
 * Created by ssalunke on 12/04/2016.
 */
public class TestRegularExpressions
{
    public static void main(String args [] )
     {
        String sampleText = "My name is Sagar. I
live in Brisbane." + "My mobile number is 9850182384
and " +"email address is reply2sagar@gmail.com. " +
 "In brisbane there are lots of Parks. I have a Car
" +"And it's registration number is QLD - 2839" ;

        //Check if above string has Brisbane in
it...No matter which case

        Pattern p =
Pattern.compile("brisbane",Pattern.CASE_INSENSITIVE)
;
        Matcher matcher = p.matcher(sampleText);
        if (matcher.find())
        {
```

```
            System.out.println("Brisbane is found in
the sampleText");
        }
        else
        {
            System.out.println("Brisbane is not
found in the sampleText");
        }

        //To find how many times, pattern (Brisbane)
is found
        // and also print position where the match
is found
        matcher.reset();
        int i=0;
        while (matcher.find())
        {
            i++;
            System.out.println("Match no " + i + "
started at "+ matcher.start() + " and ended at " +
matcher.end()+ " What found ? -> " +
matcher.group());

        }

        System.out.println("Pattern" + p.toString()
+ " was found " + i+ " times in sampleText" );

        //To see if there is a number with 10 digits
in sampleText and print that

        matcher.reset();
        p = Pattern.compile("\\d{10}");
        matcher.usePattern(p);
        i=0;
        while (matcher.find())
        {
            i++;

        System.out.println("Match no" +i+"started at
"+ matcher.start()+"and ended at"+ matcher.end()+"
What found ? -> "+matcher.group());

        }
```

```
        System.out.println("Pattern " + p.toString()
+" was found " + i + " times in sampleText" );

        //To see if there is a registration number
in sampleText and print that

        matcher.reset();
        p = Pattern.compile("(QLD)( - \\d{4})");
        matcher.usePattern(p);
        i=0;
        while (matcher.find())
        {
            i++;
            System.out.println("Match no " + i + "
started at "+ matcher.start() + " and ended at " +
matcher.end()+ " What found ? -> " +
matcher.group());

            System.out.println("Group count -> " +
matcher.groupCount() + " "+ matcher.group(1) +
matcher.group(2));

        }

        System.out.println("Pattern " + p.toString()
+" was found " + i + " times in sampleText" );

        //to see if the pattern matches with entire
sampleText
        matcher.reset();
        p = Pattern.compile(".*Parks.*");
        matcher.usePattern(p);

        if (matcher.matches())
        {
            System.out.println("Pattern" +
p.toString()+" matches entire sampleText");
        }
        else
        {
            System.out.println("Pattern" +
p.toString()+" does not match entire sampleText");
        }
```

```
        //replacing matched pattern with something
else.
        // Here Brisbane will be replaced by Sydney
        p =
Pattern.compile("brisbane",Pattern.CASE_INSENSITIVE)
;
        matcher = p.matcher(sampleText);

System.out.printf(matcher.replaceAll("Sydney"));
        //to replace first match, use replaceFirst
method
    }
}
```

**Here is the output of the above program.**

```
Brisbane is found in the sampleText
Match no 1 started at 28 and ended at 36 What
found ? -> Brisbane
Match no 2 started at 115 and ended at 123 What
found ? -> brisbane
Pattern brisbane was found 2 times in
sampleText
Match no 1 started at 57 and ended at 67 What
found ? -> 9850182384
Pattern \d{10} was found 1 times in sampleText
Match no 1 started at 194 and ended at 204 What
found ? -> QLD - 2839
Group count -> 2 QLD - 2839
Pattern (QLD)( - \d{4}) was found 1 times in
sampleText
Pattern.*Parks.* matches entire sampleText
```

```
My name is Sagar. I live in Sydney.My mobile
number is 9850182384 and email address is
reply2sagar@gmail.com. In Sydney there are lots
of Parks. I have a Car And it's registration
number is QLD - 2839
```

# 21. Input output programming in Java

## 21.1 Introduction

Input/output programming involves reading and writing to files, sockets, console etc.

For example --

System.in is a standard input stream (Keyboard) and System.out is the standard output stream (console).

Below image shows how a typical Java application reads data from InputStream of file, console or socket and writes to OutputStream of other file, socket or console.

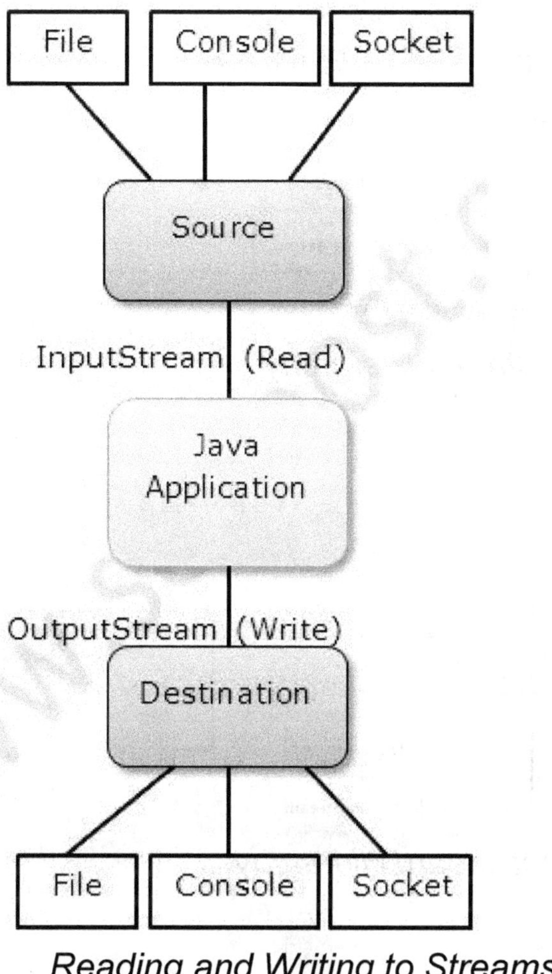


*Reading and Writing to Streams*

Below images show important classes and interfaces required for I/O programming in Java.

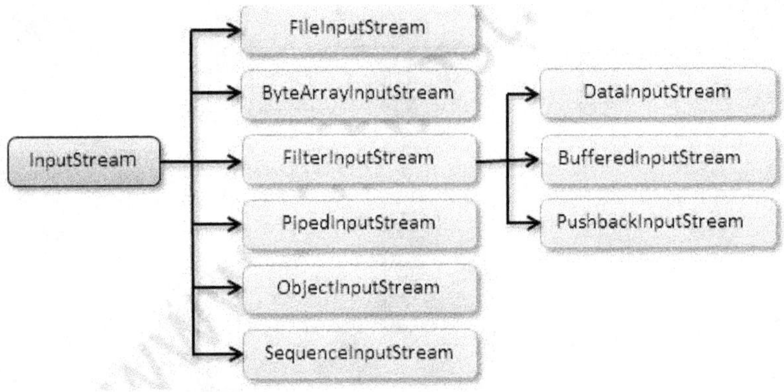


*InputStream Hierarchy*

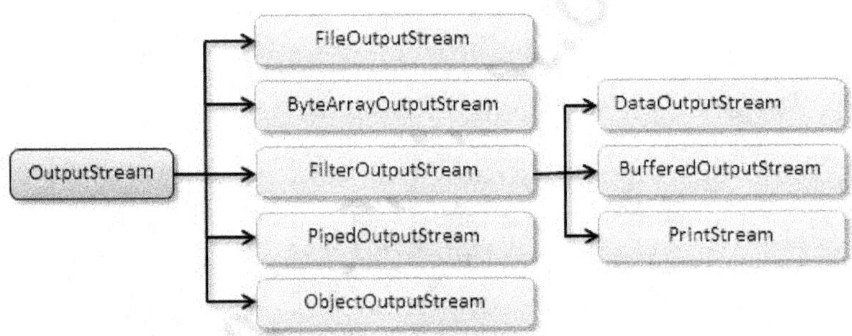


*OutputStream Hierarchy*

## 21.2 File Handling

In this article, we will learn how to work with files and directories in Java.

java.io and java.nio package contains all classes and interfaces required for working with files in Java. We can read and write from the files using FileInputStream and FileOutputStream classes respectively.

Below code will illustrate how to work with files in Java and perform basic things like checking if file exists, how to create, delete files, get more information about files in Java and read contents of file.

```
package corejava;

import org.junit.Test;
import java.io.File;
import java.io.FileWriter;
import java.io.IOException;
import java.io.PrintWriter;
import java.nio.file.Files;
import java.nio.file.Path;
import java.nio.file.Paths;

/**
 * Created by Sagar on 10-04-2016.
 */
public class files
  {

    @Test
    public void createFile()
      {
        try
         {
```

```
            //check if file exists
            String path = "f1.txt";

            File f = new File(path);

            if(f.exists() && !f.isDirectory())
             {
                 System.out.println("Using exists -
File exists");
             }
            else
             {
                 System.out.println("Using exists -
File does not exist");
             }

            //append to file. Create a file if not
exists
         FileWriter writer = new FileWriter(f,true);
            writer.append("Hello ");
            writer.flush();
            writer.close();

            if (new File(path).isFile())
            {
                 System.out.println("Using isFile -
File exists");
            }
            else
            {
                 System.out.println("Using exists -
File does not exist");
            }

            Path path1 = Paths.get(path);

            if (Files.exists(path1) &&
!Files.isDirectory(path1))
            {
                 System.out.println("Using Path -
File exists");
            }
```

```
            else
             {
                 System.out.println("Using Path -
File does not exist");
             }

             //Read all contents of a file

System.out.println(Files.readAllLines(path1));

             //deleting a file
             Files.delete(path1);

         }
        catch (IOException ex)
         {

         }
     }
}
```

**Here is the output of above program.**

```
Using exists - File does not exist
Using isFile - File exists
Using Path - File exists
[Hello ]
```

# 22. Nested Classes

There are 2 main types of nested class.

1. Static nested class
2. Non-Static nested class (Also called as Inner class)

Non-static (Inner class) classes can be divided into 3 types as mentioned below.

1. Normal
2. Method local
3. Anonymous

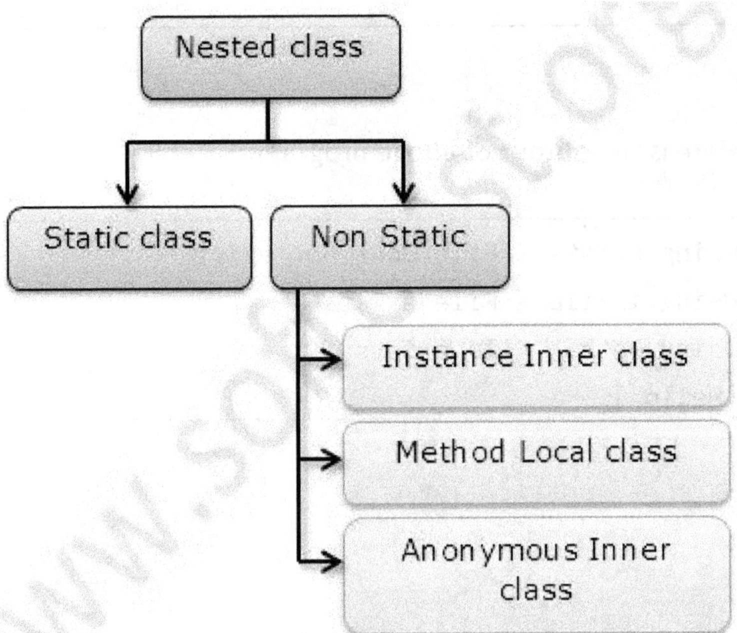

Below example will illustrate how to work with Nested classes.

```
package corejava.nestedclasses;

//Class A is an outer class
public class A
{
    private int number;
    public String name;
    static private String city;

    //class B is an inner class (Non-Static)
    class B
     {
        public void printB()
         {
            System.out.println("This is non-static
nested class " +"so it can access private members of
outer class" + name);

         }
     }

    public void hi()
     {
        //Class C is a method local inner class
        class C
        {
        }

        C c1 = new C();
     }

    //Static class
    static class D
    {
        public void print()
        {
            System.out.println("This is static inner
class");
```

```
            System.out.println("I can not access non
static " +"members of outer but can access static
memebrs" +"like city in this case");

            //We can not access class C from here
            // as it is local to method hi() of
outer class only
            //C c1 = new C();
        }
    }

    public static void main(String[] args)
    {
        D d1 = new D();
        d1.print();
    }
}
```

# 23. Collections

Collections is nothing but the group of Objects.

In Java, collection framework is made up of below classes and interfaces. Important interfaces in Collection framework are given below.

1. List - stores all types of values
2. Set - stores only unique values
3. Queue - stores values in Queue data structure
4. Map - Stores key-value pairs

Important concrete classes that implement above interfaces are given below.

1. ArrayList, LinkedList, Vector, Stack
2. HashSet, TreeSet, LinkedHashSet
3. PriorityQueue, ArrayDeque
4. HashMap, TreeMap, LinkedHashMap, HashTable, SortedMap
5. Collections - provides some static methods (algorithms) to work with any collection type
6. Iterable - This interface is used for iterating through elements in the collection object

Below image shows various classes and interfaces hierarchy of collections framework in Java.

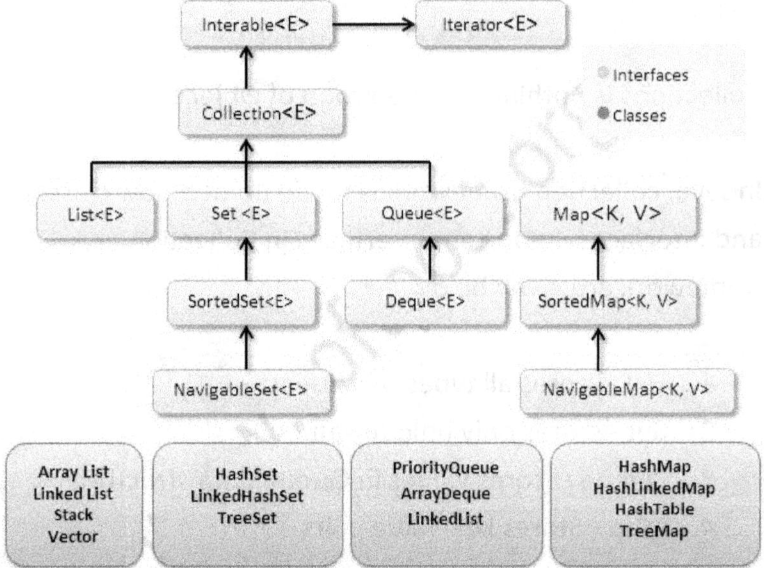


*Interfaces & Classes in Java Collections Framework*

Below image helps us to understand which collection class should be used and when.

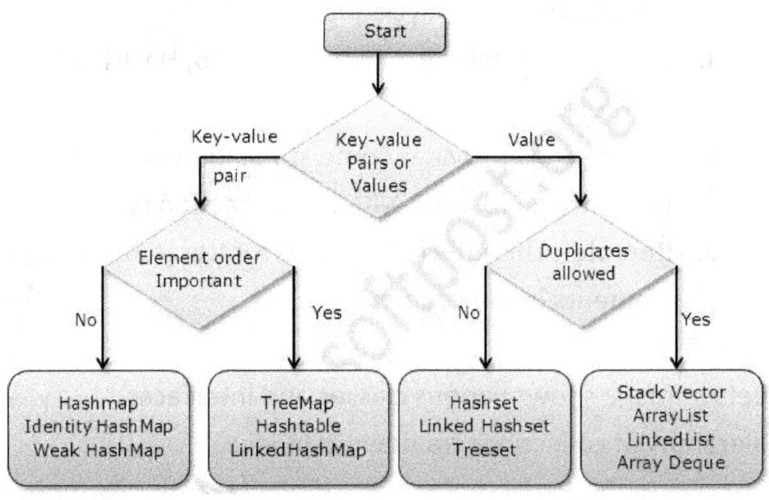

Here is an example ArrayList.

```
package corejava;

import java.util.ArrayList;
import java.util.Collections;
import java.util.Iterator;
import java.util.List;

/**
 * Created by Sagar on 10-04-2016.
 */
public class collections
{

    public static void main(String [] args)
    {
        List<String> myList = new
ArrayList<String>();
        myList.add("Brisbane");
        myList.add("Paris");
        myList.add("chicago");
        myList.add("London");
        Collections.sort(myList);

        //Iterating using new for loop
        for (String x : myList)
        {
            System.out.println(x);
        }

        myList.remove("Paris");
        System.out.println("*********After removing
Paris*********");
        //Iterating using Itr class
        Iterator<String> iter = myList.iterator();

        while (iter.hasNext())
        {
```

```
            String str = iter.next();
            System.out.println(str);
        }
        System.out.println("List size is -> " +
myList.size());

        System.out.println("List contains London? ->
" + myList.contains("London"));

      //Iterating using Lambda expressions in Java 8
myList.forEach( value -> System.out.println(value));

    }
}
```

**Here is the output of the above code.**

```
Brisbane
London
Paris
chicago
*********After removing Paris*********
Brisbane
London
chicago
List size is -> 3
List contains London? -> true
Brisbane
London
chicago


Process finished with exit code 0
```

# 24. Generics

Generics solves 2 problems -

1. Type casting
2. Type safety

Explanation - Normal ArrayList class is not generic. We can store any type of object in same ArrayList which causes type casting and type safety problems.

ArrayList a = new ArrayList();

But In Generic ArrayList, we can store only specific types. For example, in below ArrayList instance, we can only store String objects.

ArrayList<String> a = new ArrayList<>();

```
package generics;

/**
 * Created by ssalunke on 15/04/2016.
 */

//Without Generics, we will have to create 2
different Classes each working with specific Type
say Water and Petrol. Here note that <G> is a type
of Parameter.

public class MyGenericClass <G>
{
```

```
    G liquid;
    public static void main(String [] args)
    {
        MyGenericClass<Water> w = new
MyGenericClass<>();
        w.liquid = new Water();

        MyGenericClass<Petrol> p = new
MyGenericClass<>();
        p.liquid = new Petrol();

    }
}


class Water
{
}

class Petrol
{
}
```

**Bounded Types in Generics**

Bounded types allow us to restrict the types to specific set of classes. For example - Mathematical operations can be performed only on Classes inherited by Number class. So we can restrict the types using extends keyword. In below example, we can create instance of BoundedTypes class using only **Number Type or it's child classes.**

```
package generics;

/**
 * Created by ssalunke on 15/04/2016.
 */

//Bounded types are required when we need to work
with specific types only
//For example - if we have a generic class that does
mathematical operations
//then we should restrict the types using Bounded
types
public class BoundedTypes <T extends Number>
   {

    public void add(T a, T b){
        System.out.println("Sum of numbers is " +
(a.doubleValue()+b.doubleValue()));
   }

    public void multiply(T a, T b)
     {
        System.out.println("Multiplication of
numbers is " + (a.doubleValue()*b.doubleValue()));
     }

    public static void main(String [] args)
     {
        BoundedTypes<Integer> intTypes = new
BoundedTypes<>();
        intTypes.add(11,22);
        intTypes.multiply(11,22);

        BoundedTypes<Float> floatTypes = new
BoundedTypes<>();
        floatTypes.add(32.2f,22.4f);

        BoundedTypes<Double> doubleTypes = new
BoundedTypes<>();
        doubleTypes.add(132.2d,222.4d);

    }
}
```

**Here is the output of above code.**

```
Sum of numbers is 33.0
Multiplication of numbers is 242.0
Sum of numbers is 54.60000038146973
Sum of numbers is 354.6
```

# 25. Serialization

In this topic, we will learn what is Serialization, how we can achieve it and what are the advantages of it.

Serialization is nothing but storing the object on disk, memory or database in the form of bytes. Main advantage of Serialization is that we can restore the object in future. The reverse process of getting object from disk or file is called as Deserialization.

Remember that transient members are not saved during Serialization process.

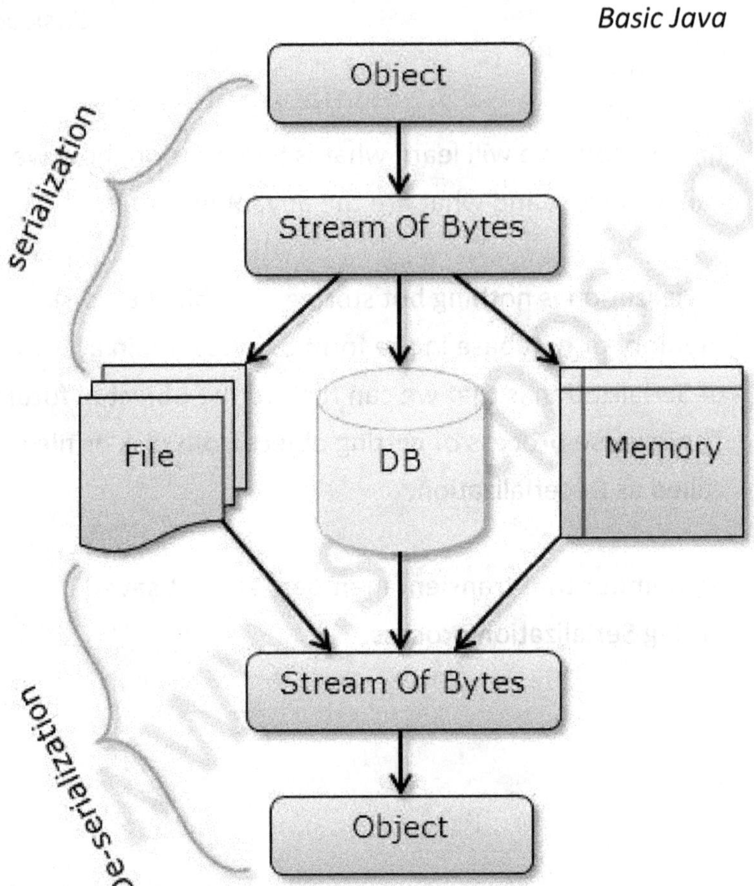


*Serialization and Deserialization*

Below example illustrates how we can perform Serialization and Deserialization.

```
package serialization;

/**
 * Created by ssalunke on 12/04/2016.
 */
import java.io.*;

public class Serialization
{
```

```
    public static void main(String [] args)
    {
        Student student = new Student();
        student.name = "Sagar Salunke";
        student.rollno = 10;
        student.tempNo = 111;

        try
        {
            FileOutputStream fileOut = new
FileOutputStream("student.obj");
            ObjectOutputStream out = new
ObjectOutputStream(fileOut);
            out.writeObject(student);
            out.close();
            fileOut.close();
            System.out.println("Student object will
be stored in student.obj file");
        }
       catch(IOException i)
        {
            i.printStackTrace();
        }
    }
}

class DeserializeStudent
{
    public static void main(String [] args)
    {
        Student student = null;
        try
        {
            FileInputStream fileIn = new
FileInputStream("student.obj");
            ObjectInputStream in = new
ObjectInputStream(fileIn);
            student = (Student) in.readObject();
            in.close();
            fileIn.close();
        }
       catch(IOException i)
        {
            i.printStackTrace();
```

```
            return;
        }
       catch(ClassNotFoundException c)
        {
            System.out.println("Student class not
found");
            c.printStackTrace();
            return;
        }

        System.out.println("Deserialized
Student...");
        System.out.println("Name -> " +
student.name);
        System.out.println("Roll no -> " +
student.rollno);
        System.out.println("Temp no -> " +
student.tempNo);

    }
}

class Student implements java.io.Serializable
{
    //transient members will not be saved
    public int rollno;
    public String name;
    public transient int tempNo;
}
```

**Here is the output of first program - Serialization**

```
Student object will be stored in student.obj
file
```

```
Here is the output of second program -
Deserialization

Deserialized Student...
Name -> Sagar Salunke
Roll no -> 10
Temp no -> 0
```

# 26. Socket programming

There are 2 types of sockets in Java.

1. ServerSocket - TCP
2. DatagramSocket - UDP

Communicating over tcp/udp is possible through ServerSocket class.

Server socket will do below tasks.

1. Create a Server Socket using ServerSocket Class
2. Then call accept() method to wait for connections
3. Then read and write to sockets i/p & o/p streams

Client socket will do below tasks.

1. Connect to server using below syntax
2. Socket client = new Socket(serverName, port);
3. Then read and write to socket using i/p & o/p streams

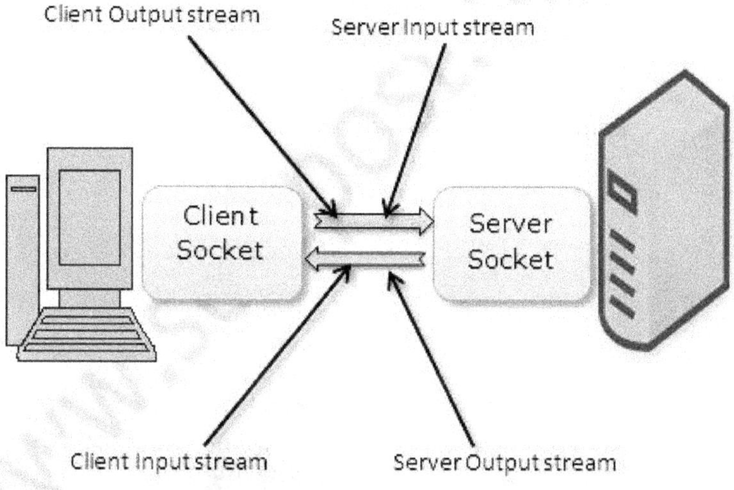


Here is the sample Java program which illustrates socket programming.

Here is the server code.

```
package sockets;

/**
 * Created by ssalunke on 12/04/2016.
 */
import java.net.*;
import java.io.*;

public class Server extends Thread
{

    public static void main(String[] args) throws
Exception
    {
```

```
        System.out.println("Server Listening on 
8888");
        ServerSocket serverSocket = new 
ServerSocket(8888);
        //server timeout 60 minutes
        serverSocket.setSoTimeout(1000 * 60 * 60);

        //Below method waits until client socket 
tries to connect
        Socket server = serverSocket.accept();

        //Read from client using input stream
        DataInputStream in = new 
DataInputStream(server.getInputStream());
        System.out.println(in.readUTF());

        //Write to client using output stream
        DataOutputStream out = new 
DataOutputStream(server.getOutputStream());
        out.writeUTF("Bye sent by Server");

        //close the connection
        server.close();
    }
}
Here is the client code
package sockets;

import java.net.*;
import java.io.*;

public class Client
{
    public static void main(String[] args) throws 
Exception
    {

        //try to connect to server - localhost @ 
port 8888
       Socket client = new Socket("localhost",8888);

        //if server is not listening - You will get 
Exception
```

```
        // java.net.ConnectException: Connection
refused: connect

        //write to server using output stream
        DataOutputStream out = new
DataOutputStream(client.getOutputStream());

        out.writeUTF("Hello server - How are you
sent by Client");

        //read from the server
        DataInputStream in = new
DataInputStream(client.getInputStream());

        System.out.println("Data received from the
server is -> " + in.readUTF());

        //close the connection
        client.close();
    }
}
```

**Please run the server code first then run client code.**

Here is the server output.

```
Server Listening on 8888
Hello server - How are you sent by Client

Here is the client output.
Data received from the server is -> Bye sent by
Server
```

# 27. Multi-Threading

There are 2 ways in which we can do multi-tasking in computer systems.

1. Process based multi-tasking
2. Thread based multi-tasking

Java has a very good support for multi-threading based multi-tasking. Multi threading is used when you need to execute the independent jobs within same program simultaneously.

Usually, our code is run in sequential manner - one line at a time. There is just a single flow (Also called as Main Thread). With threads, we can have multiple flows of the execution. Remember that Multi-threading is mostly useful in scenarios where we have multiple independent jobs.

## 28.1 Thread Life Cycle

A thread follows typical life cycle as shown in below image. Start() method invokes run method and thread is put in running state. Thread can go into not running state due to many reasons as mentioned below.

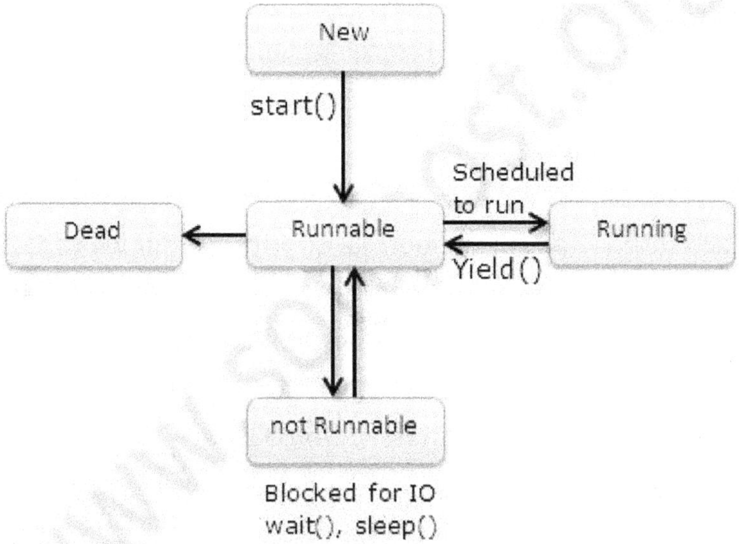


1. sleep method is called (Stops the execution of current thread for specific duration)
2. yield method is called (Suspends execution of current thread and gives other threads a chance to run)
3. wait method is called (Waits for other thread to release a lock)
4. join method is called (waits until other thread finishes execution)
5. waiting for I/O operation to finish

A thread will start running once any of the above operation is complete. Thread scheduler decides which thread has to be started and when.

Each thread dies at the end of cycle and goes to dead state.

**Thread Priority**

Each thread has got the normal priority (5). But we can change the priority of thread. Suppose there are 2 thread t1 and t2. You want to run t2 before t1. Then you will have to set the t2's priority higher than t1. If we set t2's priority as 6, then t2 will run before t1

## 28.2 Creating a thread

There are 2 ways in which we can create threads in Java.

1. By extending Thread class
2. By implementing Runnable interface

Difference between these 2 approaches is that when we create a thread by extending a Thread, we can not extend any other class thus we can not use inheritance in first method. While in second method, we can extend any other class.

**Threads by extending the Thread class.**

In this approach, we have to create a class which extends a thread and then create a run method in it which performs a specific job. Let us say we need to perform 2 tasks - print squares of 1 - 10 and print cubes of 1 - 10. So Both the jobs are independent of each other. We can have first thread printing squares and other thread printing cubes simultaneously.

```
package corejava;

/**
 * Created by Sagar on 10-04-2016.
 */
public class ThreadingClass
{

    public static void main(String [] args)
    {
        SquareThread t1 = new SquareThread();
        CubeThread t2 = new CubeThread();
        t1.start();
        t2.start();
    }
}

class SquareThread extends Thread
{
    public void run()
    {
        for (int i=1;i<=10;i++)
         {
            System.out.println("SquareThread -> " +
i*i);
        }
    }
}

class CubeThread extends Thread
{
    public void run()
     {
        for (int i=1;i<=10;i++)
        {
            System.out.println("CubeThread -> " +
i*i*i);
```

```
        }
    }
}
```

**Here is the sample output of above code.**

```
SquareThread -> 1
SquareThread -> 4
SquareThread -> 9
SquareThread -> 16
CubeThread -> 1
SquareThread -> 25
CubeThread -> 8
SquareThread -> 36
CubeThread -> 27
SquareThread -> 49
CubeThread -> 64
SquareThread -> 64
CubeThread -> 125
SquareThread -> 81
CubeThread -> 216
SquareThread -> 100
CubeThread -> 343
CubeThread -> 512
CubeThread -> 729
CubeThread -> 1000


Process finished with exit code 0
```

**Threads by implementing Runnable interface.**

```
package corejava;
/**
 * Created by Sagar on 10-04-2016.
 */
public class ThreadingByRunnable
{
    public static void main(String [] args)
    {
        NewSquareThread st = new NewSquareThread();
        Thread t1 = new Thread(st);
        NewCubeThread ct = new NewCubeThread();
        Thread t2 = new Thread(ct);
        t1.start();
        t2.start();
    }
}

class NewSquareThread implements Runnable
{
    public void run()
    {
        for (int i=1;i<=10;i++)
        {
            System.out.println("NewSquareThread -> "
+ i*i);
        }
    }
}

class NewCubeThread implements Runnable
{
    public void run()
    {
        for (int i=1;i<=10;i++)
        {
            System.out.println("NewCubeThread -> " +
i*i*i);
        }
    }
}
```

## 28. Annotations

Annotations can be used to give special instructions to program in Java. There are 3 types of annotations in Java.

1. Compiler  Annotations
2. Build time Annotations
3. Runtime Annotations (e.g. @Test in Junit Framework)

Annotations are marked by @ symbol. We can annotate classes, methods, variables, interfaces and constructors.

Built-in Annotations in Java.

1. @Override
2. @SuppressWarnings
3. @Deprecated

You must have noticed these annotations while working in any JAVA IDE like eclipse or intellij IDEA. These annotations are automatically added at appropriate places. For example – if compiler thinks that some method is old, it inserts @Deprecated annotation above the method. We can also annotate method with @Override if you are overriding that method. To supress warnings in a class, you can use @SuppressWarnings annotation.

```
package annotations;

import jdk.nashorn.internal.ir.annotations.Ignore;
import org.junit.Test;

import java.lang.annotation.ElementType;
import java.lang.annotation.Retention;
import java.lang.annotation.RetentionPolicy;
import java.lang.annotation.Target;

/**
 * Created by ssalunke on 13/04/2016.
 */
public class TestAnnotations
{

    @Test(timeout = 1000) @Ignore
    public void test()
    {
        System.out.println("Standard JUnit Test 
annotation");
    }

    @MyTest(myIgnore = "Yes",myPriority = 2)
    public void testMyAnnotation()
    {
        System.out.println("Custom Annotation ");
    }
}

@Retention(RetentionPolicy.RUNTIME)
@Target({ElementType.METHOD,ElementType.CONSTRUCTOR}
)
@interface MyTest
{
    String   myIgnore() default "";
    int      myPriority() default 1;
}
```

# 29. Lambda Expressions

Lambda expressions were introduced in Java 8. They are also called as anonymous methods.

Below example explains how we can use Lambda expressions.

```
package lambda;

/**
 * Created by ssalunke on 14/04/2016.
 */

interface Executable
{
    public void execute();
}

interface OtherExecutable
{
    public void executeOther(int a);
}

class X
{
    //all that test method needs is block of code
    //as per the interface Executable
    public void test(Executable e)
    {
        e.execute();
    }

    public void testOther(OtherExecutable e)
    {
        e.executeOther(10);
    }
}
```

```
public class Lambda
{

    public static void main(String [] args)
   {
        X x1 = new X();

        //here we are passing the implementation of
execute method
        x1.test(new Executable()
         {
            @Override
            public void execute()
            {
                System.out.println("Execute code
using legacy code");
            }
        });

        //here we are passing the implementation of
execute using lambda expression
        x1.test(()->
                {
                    System.out.println("hi");
                    System.out.println("It's lambda
expression");
                }

        );

        x1.testOther((a) -> System.out.println("This
lambda takes in 1 int parameter a -> " + a) );

    }

}
```

# 30. Reflections in Java

With reflections, we can get the information about any class's structure like its methods, fields, constructors etc. We can also create the instances of the classes at run time and invoke its methods.

For example - Let us say we have a Student class in Java and we want to find all method and fields of that class.

```
package reflections;

/**
 * Created by ssalunke on 13/04/2016.
 */

public class Student
{

    private int rollno;
    private String name;
    public int marks;

    public Student(int rn, String name, int marks)
    {
        this.rollno = rn;
        this.name = name;
        this.marks = marks;
    }

    public Student (int rn, String name)
    {
        this.rollno = rn;
        this.name = name;
        this.marks = 0;
    }
```

```
    public Student (int rn)
    {
        this.rollno = rn;
        this.name = "";
        this.marks = 0;
    }

    public int getMarks()
    {
        return marks;
    }

    public int getRollno()
    {
        return rollno;
    }


    public String getName()
    {
        return name;
    }

    public void setMarks(int marks)
    {
        this.marks = marks;
    }

    public void setName(String name)
    {
        this.name = name;
    }

}
```

## Finding field information of Student class

```
package reflections;

import org.junit.Test;
import java.lang.reflect.Field;

/**
 * Created by ssalunke on 13/04/2016.
 */
public class TestFields
{

    @Test
    public void testField() throws Exception
    {
        Class studentClass = Student.class;

        Student s1 = new Student(11,"Sagar");

        // gets all the public member fields of the
class Student
        Field[] fields = studentClass.getFields();

        System.out.println("Public Fields are: ");
        for (Field oneField : fields)
        {
            // get public field name
            Field field =
studentClass.getField(oneField.getName());

            String fieldname = field.getName();
            System.out.println("Fieldname is: " +
fieldname);

            // get public field type
            Object fieldType = field.getType();
            System.out.println("Type of field " +
fieldname + " is: "+ fieldType);
```

```
            // get public field value
            Object value = field.get(s1);
            System.out.println("Value of field " +
fieldname + " is: "+ value);

        }

        // How to access private member fields of
the class

        // getDeclaredField() returns the private
field
        Field privateField =
Student.class.getDeclaredField("name");

        String name = privateField.getName();
        System.out.println("One private Fieldname
is: " + name);
        // makes this private field instance
accessible
        // for reflection use only, not normal code
        privateField.setAccessible(true);

        // get the value of this private field
        String fieldValue = (String)
privateField.get(s1);
        System.out.println("fieldValue = " +
fieldValue);

    }
}
```

**Here is the output of Above Java program.**

```
Public Fields are:
Fieldname is: marks
Type of field marks is: int
```

```
Value of field marks is: 0
One private Fieldname is: name
fieldValue = Sagar
```

**Now let us try to find method information of Student class.**

```
package reflections;

import java.lang.reflect.Constructor;
import java.lang.reflect.Field;
import java.lang.reflect.InvocationTargetException;
import java.lang.reflect.Method;
import java.util.Arrays;

/**
 * Created by ssalunke on 13/04/2016.
 */
public class TestMethods
  {

    public static void main(String[] args) throws
Exception
    {

        Class studentClass = Student.class;

            // get the name of the class including
package name
        System.out.println("Class Name (including
package) is -> " + studentClass.getName());

            // get the name of the class excluding
package
        System.out.println("Class Name (excluding
package) is -> " + studentClass.getSimpleName());

        System.out.println("Package Name of the
class is -> " + studentClass.getPackage());
```

```
            // get all the constructors of the class
            Constructor[] constructors =
studentClass.getConstructors();
            System.out.println("Constructors are: "
+ Arrays.toString(constructors));

            // get constructor with specific
argument
            Constructor constructor =
studentClass.getConstructor(Integer.TYPE);

            // initializing an object of the RentCar
class
            Student s1 = (Student)
constructor.newInstance(111);

            // get all methods of the class
including declared methods of superclasses
    Method[] allmethods = studentClass.getMethods();
    System.out.println("Methods are: " +
Arrays.toString(allmethods));

     for (Method method : allmethods)
     {
                System.out.println("method = " +
method.getName());
     }

            // get all methods declared in the class
but excludes inherited methods.
        Method[] declaredMethods =
studentClass.getDeclaredMethods();
        System.out.println("Declared Methods are: "
+ Arrays.toString(declaredMethods));

        for (Method dmethod : declaredMethods)
         {
                System.out.println("method = " +
dmethod.getName());
         }

            // get method with specific name and
parameters
```

```
     Method oneMethod =
studentClass.getMethod("setName",
     new Class[]{String.class});

     System.out.println("Method is: " + oneMethod);

     oneMethod.invoke(s1, "Sagar");

             // get all the parameters of setName
     Class[] parameterTypes =
oneMethod.getParameterTypes();
     System.out.println("Parameter types of setName
are: "+ Arrays.toString(parameterTypes));

             // get the return type of setName
     Class returnType = oneMethod.getReturnType();

 System.out.println("Return type is: " +returnType);

    }
}
```

**Here is the output of above program.**

```
Class Name (including package) is ->
reflections.Student
Class Name (excluding package) is -> Student
Package Name of the class is -> package
reflections
Constructors are: [public
reflections.Student(int), public
reflections.Student(int,java.lang.String),
public
reflections.Student(int,java.lang.String,int)]
```

```
Methods are: [public java.lang.String
reflections.Student.getName(), public void
reflections.Student.setName(java.lang.String),
public int reflections.Student.getMarks(),
public int reflections.Student.getRollno(),
public void reflections.Student.setMarks(int),
public final void java.lang.Object.wait()
throws java.lang.InterruptedException, public
final void java.lang.Object.wait(long,int)
throws java.lang.InterruptedException, public
final native void java.lang.Object.wait(long)
throws java.lang.InterruptedException, public
boolean
java.lang.Object.equals(java.lang.Object),
public java.lang.String
java.lang.Object.toString(), public native int
java.lang.Object.hashCode(), public final
native java.lang.Class
java.lang.Object.getClass(), public final
native void java.lang.Object.notify(), public
final native void java.lang.Object.notifyAll()]
method = getName
method = setName
method = getMarks
method = getRollno
method = setMarks
method = wait
method = wait
method = wait
```

```
method = equals
method = toString
method = hashCode
method = getClass
method = notify
method = notifyAll
Declared Methods are: [public java.lang.String
reflections.Student.getName(), public void
reflections.Student.setName(java.lang.String),
public int reflections.Student.getMarks(),
public int reflections.Student.getRollno(),
public void reflections.Student.setMarks(int)]
method = getName
method = setName
method = getMarks
method = getRollno
method = setMarks
Method is: public void
reflections.Student.setName(java.lang.String)
Parameter types of setName are: [class
java.lang.String]
Return type is: void
```

# 31. Singleton class in Java

Singleton is a class wherein we can create just a single object of that class. Runtime is one of the most important built-in Singleton class in Java library. But we can also create our custom singleton class as shown in below example. Note that we can create only one instance of that class.

```
package singleton;

import org.junit.Test;

/**
 * Created by ssalunke on 13/04/2016.
 */

public class TestSingleTon
{

    @Test
    public void test()
    {

System.out.println(SingleTon.getInstance().hashCode(
));

        //Below statement will throw compile time
error
        //Runtime r = new Runtime();

        //Below statement will throw compile time
error
        //SingleTon s1 = new SingleTon();

    }
}
```

```
class SingleTon
{

    private static SingleTon instance = null;

    private SingleTon()
     {
            // This constructor is private which
means that
            //we can not create objects using new
Operator
    }

    public static SingleTon getInstance()
     {
        if (instance == null)
        {
            instance = new SingleTon();
        }
        return instance;
    }
}
```

# 32. Runtime Class in Java

Runtime is a singleton class in Java. You can perform below tasks using Runtime class.

1. Execute any OS command – exec()
2. Find free memory – freeMemory()
3. Find total memory – totalMemory()
4. Terminate the Java application – exit()
5. Get the count of processors available to JVM – availableProcessors()

Below example demonstrates Runtime usage.

```
package runtime;

/**
 * Created by Sagar on 16-04-2016.
 */
public class RuntimeTest
{

    public static void main(String [] args)throws
Exception
    {
        Runtime runtime=Runtime.getRuntime();
        System.out.println("Count of Processors ->
"+runtime.availableProcessors());

        System.out.println("Total Memory ->
"+runtime.totalMemory());

        System.out.println("Free Memory ->
"+runtime.freeMemory());
```

```
        //Launch calculator using exec. You can
execute any command using exec

Process calculatorProcess =runtime.exec("calc.exe");
        //Program will continue running until you
close the calculator
        calculatorProcess.waitFor();
        runtime.exit(0);

    }
}
```

**Here is the sample output of above code.**

```
Count of Processors -> 4
Total Memory -> 56623104
Free Memory -> 54190136
```

www.ingramcontent.com/pod-product-compliance
Lightning Source LLC
Chambersburg PA
CBHW071129050326
40690CB00008B/1391

* 9 7 8 1 5 3 3 0 5 3 5 0 3 *